CATO STREET

By

ROBERT SHAW

1972
CHATTO & WINDUS
LONDON

Published by
Chatto and Windus Ltd
40 William IV Street
London WC2N 4DF

*

Clarke, Irwin and Co Ltd
Toronto

ISBN 0 7011 1878 4

Printed in Great Britain by
Redwood Press Ltd
Trowbridge, Wiltshire

For Thornton Wilder
For Bert Knapp

Clothed with the Bible, as with light
And the shadows of the night
Like Sidmouth, next Hypocrisy,
On a crocodile rode by.

October. 1819.
Shelley

Author's Note: The leading conspirators in the
Cato Street plot was in fact,
a man - Arthur Thistlewood. I
have changed him into a woman
because his wife Susan was,
according to the historian E.P.
Thompson, "a spirited Jacobin
in her own right"; and because
I feel it is more interesting for
the audience to have a woman
to look at. The women of 1819
were active in the Radical
movement.
Hannah Smith was hanged
before 1819.

LIST OF CHARACTERS

MRS. SUSAN THISTLEWOOD
HARRY THISTLEWOOD
WILLIAM DAVIDSON
HANNAH SMITH
ORATOR HUNT
A LIEUTENANT
A CONSTABLE
THE HOME SECRETARY - LORD SIDMOUTH
LORD SIDMOUTH'S PRIVATE SECRETARY - HERBERT
THOMAS BRUNT
JAMES INGS
RICHARD TIDD
WILLIAM COBBETT
THE VERY OLD MAN - LORD WILKINSON
SIR FRANCIS BURDETT
MONSIEUR MABEUF
A DRUNKEN IRISHMAN
ELLEN COX
ROBERT ADAMS
PALIN
WALTER GILCHRIST
MRS. EDWARDS
A BABY
THE CONSTABLE RUTHVEN
MARY EDWARDS
SMITHERS
THE LORD CHIEF JUSTICE
THE REVEREND MR. COTTON
THE "DOCTOR"
HAROLD WALTERS
THE POOR MAN

MEN, WOMEN, CHILDREN, CONSTABLES, SOLDIERS, JUSTICES, and a CRIER etc., appear and speak at various times.

ACT ONE

*England, 1819, Monday afternoon; St.
Peter's Fields, a piece of vacant land in
Manchester — the stage is bare with a
Church on the back-cloth.*

*Sitting on the ground eating bread and
cheese are SUSAN THISTLEWOOD, her
fourteen year old son, HARRY, and the
Negro, WILLIAM DAVIDSON. They eat
in silence. Far away a bugle blows.*

SUSAN:	It's on then.
DAVIDSON:	I hope it don't rain.
SUSAN:	*(looking at the sky)* It won't rain today.
HARRY:	I've got bad blisters, Mum.
SUSAN:	It's those shoes.
DAVIDSON:	Yes.
SUSAN:	When I was a girl I could have done it barefoot.
HARRY:	You said that.
SUSAN:	When I was a girl.

(A bugle blows nearer)

HARRY:	Do you think there'll be trouble?
SUSAN:	No.
HARRY:	What if they get out soldiers?
SUSAN:	They won't
HARRY:	What do you really think of Mr. Hunt?
SUSAN:	Speaks well.
HARRY:	I don't like him. *(pause)* It won't be the first time they've got 'em out.
SUSAN:	Hunt draws the crowds, don't he?
HARRY:	No iron in him.
DAVIDSON:	Not like your dad Arthur.

HARRY;   He's too dandy.

SUSAN: I hope they *don't* get out the soldiers!

DAVIDSON: *(taking out a book)* If they're to do that why let us meet in the first place?

HARRY: Why, to make an example of course.

SUSAN;   We've got to be peaceable or we'll get nowhere. That's what I kept telling your father. Can't fight muskets with sticks. *(pause)* I must wash my hair tonight.

(Pause)

DAVIDSON: *(reading)* "True freedom lies where a man receives his nourishment and preservation".

HARRY: Have you got blisters, Willy?

DAVIDSON: No.

HARRY: Do you think white feet blister easier than black?

DAVIDSON: I do.

SUSAN: Willy, you'll put that book away when there's company.

DAVIDSON: Of course, my love.

SUSAN: I don't want *you* taken. *(pause)* I must wash my hair tonight. *(pause)* We walked in wooded valleys. There were forests. Wild roses grew and we could kneel and drink the rindle.

HARRY: *You* should speak.

SUSAN: No. They don't like women speakers. *(pause)* No. Not me. *(pause)* There was honeysuckle and lavender.

HARRY: You must have been beautiful, Mum, in the lavender.

DAVIDSON: Beautiful now.

SUSAN: No. I've lost my looks.

DAVIDSON: Not true, my love.

SUSAN: It *is* true and you know it.

DAVIDSON: *(putting away his pamphlet)* Susie, you are the rose of Sharon and the lily of the valleys.

SUSAN: I'm no lily.

DAVIDSON: "Thou art all, fair, my love. There is no spot in thee".

SUSAN: You put too much trust in that damned Bible of yours. It'll do you in yet, that Bible. *(she smiles)* Old black bloody flatterer, aren't you!

DAVIDSON: *(grinning)* I am black but comely.

SUSAN: Yes, you are. But *my* looks have gone.

HARRY: Mother, don't keep saying that. I hate it when you say that.

(Pause)

SUSAN: Harry, when I was a girl the birds sang everywhere but now we live in a million sewage rows, we hear no birds, we see no trees, and the only water to wash with comes down filthy walls. All over this land foulness and black alleys. The poor are begging bread and milk at every corner but the rich grow rich and richer.

DAVIDSON: There's no doubt of that.

HARRY: Cheer up, Mum. It's a lovely day.

SUSAN: It is. I'm sorry to be down, my love. I'm sorry.

DAVIDSON: Tonight you'll wash your hair.

SUSAN: I'm missing Arthur.

HARRY: We know that.

SUSAN: We should never have come up here. All this way for what. We should have stayed in London, and kept out of such things.

DAVIDSON: You'll never be able to keep out, Susie.

SUSAN: *(Tearfully)* Oh God, I do feel terrible.

> (HANNAH SMITH *enters bearing a red flag inscribed "Let Women Die Like Men and Not Be Sold As Slaves", on the one side, and on the other, "Equal Representation or Death".)*

HANNAH: How do.

SUSAN: *(pulling herself together)* That's a good flag.

HANNAH: It is.

SUSAN: It's on then?

HANNAH: Permission's been granted. Though some say the soldiers are out. Come long way?

SUSAN: London. Wasn't born there though!

HANNAH: That's a tidy walk. Going to speak?

SUSAN: I don't feel like speaking.

DAVIDSON: She'll speak.

HANNAH: Hannah Smith. How do. Who's this blackie?

DAVIDSON: William Davidson.

SUSAN: Susie Thistlewood. This is my son, Harry.

HARRY: So they say the military's out.

HANNAH: Aye.

HARRY: I told you Mum, didn't I?

> *(The bugle blows again and now we hear the sound of many marching feet)*

HANNAH: Are you widow, then?

SUSAN: I am.

HANNAH: I'm widow. Widow Smith. Husband transported. Sidmouth's game laws. Taking rabbit. One rabbit for the family pot. My family. He's for Australia now if he's living. Two kids dead. Couldn't feed 'em. Yes, Tom'll be playin' with those sheep! *(she laughs)* No good

thinkin' on it. What I live for: Sidmouth's
death.

SUSAN: That's not enough to live for.

HARRY: He hanged my father.

HANNAH: Sidmouth?

SUSAN: "Incitement", they called it.

DAVIDSON: Old butcher — doctor Sidmouth. The leper.
Oh God in heaven what will you say when you
meet that hypocrite?

(Pause)

SUSAN: But you know, Hannah, we can't do nothing
that's good but through Parliament. That's
why I'm here today.

HANNAH: Never do nothing for us.

SUSAN: They will if we can vote 'em out. *(pause)* We've
got to get that vote if we die for it. All of us.

(Pause)

HANNAH: Aye. That's the truth, Susie. Somethin' in
common then, dear love. No blackie though
to comfort *me*.

SUSAN: *(smiling)* Yes, you could do with a dusky
brother.

HANNAH: Two. Two! Wonder if my Tom's got a dusky
sister. Probably drowned in boat. Got blackies
down there, haven't they?

DAVIDSON: I believe so.

HANNAH: Cannibals?

DAVIDSON: That he will have to ascertain for himself.
Come on, Missis, I'll give you a kiss.

HANNAH: After all this time I want more than that.

(DAVIDSON and HANNAH kiss)

Buy you a pint tonight?

SUSAN: Thank you. *(she smiles)* You're friendly.

HANNAH: Oh, I'm friendly.

DAVIDSON: *(grinning)* You're friendly.

HANNAH: *(to* MRS. THISTLEWOOD *)* Don't sleep as well as I did. You?

SUSAN: No.

HANNAH: Not the same is it?

SUSAN: It's not.

HANNAH: Not in the middle of the night. Can't get off, can you?

SUSAN: I find it very hard.

> *(The bugle blows loudly:* A BODY OF WORKERS *carrying a banner surmounted by a cap of Liberty; "Annual Parliament and Universal Suffrage" is written upon one side of the banner: 'Manchester Union' upon the other. They sweep on-to the stage bearing the Orator:* HENRY HUNT' *on a platform.* HUNT *wears a white top-hat.*

HANNAH: Three times three cheers for the lovely Henry Hunt.

> *(The crowd cheers loudly)*

HUNT: Gentlemen. Lancastrians. Mancunians
> *(Laughter)*
Fellow Countrymen. Patriots.

HANNAH: Patriots Not satisfied with potatoes.

HUNT: Every man wishing to hear must keep himself silent.

> *(Cheers. Various* WOMEN *shout "We are not satisfied with potatoes* MR. HUNT.*")*

HUNT: If any person is not quiet be so good as to put them down and keep them quiet.

HANNAH: All right then, shut up!

HUNT: Thank you. Indulge me now with calm and
          patient attention. It may be impossible for me
          to make myself heard by every member of this
          tremendous meeting but let those that hear me
          remember and pass the word. I do not think I
          need to recall to you the proceedings of the last
          ten days — you are acquainted with why our
          former meeting was postponed — it is therefore
          superfluous for me to say anything about that
          unless indeed it is this: Those who attempted to
          put down our first meeting by their most malig-
          nant exertions have occasioned you good people
          to meet here today in more than two-fold
          numbers; what our enemies had thought to be
          victory they can see is palpable defeat.

                      (Cheers from the crowd)

HUNT: And so now . . . now! We can get to the business
          of the day which is . . . which *is* to consider what
          are the most legal and effectual means of obtain-
          ing a Reform in the Commons Houses of Parlia-
          ment. Item one: How are the Poor to become
          Rich? Our opponents are the Government of
          the country.

                      *(Applause: shouts of "No more
                      interruptions". Shouts of "Our
                      opponents are the Government
                      of the country")*

HANNAH: Worst opponent is Home Secretary
          Sidmouth.

SUSAN: *(shouts)* It's not violence we need. It's votes.

HUNT: The only true remedy for all our ills is a reformed
          Parliament. You who they call a mob, a rabble,
          a scum, a swinish multitude — But you also who

HUNT:
(contd)

pay taxes — you who work sixteen hours a day
... you who have fought for your country ...

> *(But now a drum is heard and
> the crowd begins to mutter:
> "The Yeomanry. The Cavalry".
> Long pause)*

Be calm. They can mean us no hurt. I offered to
give myself up to the authorities before this
meeting. The magistrates here in Manchester
refused my offer. You are allowed to assemble.
The Riot Act has not been read. Soldiers! We
have permission to assemble! The Riot Act has
not been read!

> *(The* SOLDIERS *continue to
> approach, led by a* DRUMMER*)*

Three cheers for our soldiers!

> *(The crowd does cheer but
> since the* SOLDIERS *do not
> cease their advance the crowd
> falls silent and packs close)*

Lieutenant, you will see this is no rabble. Only
the aged and the infirm are carrying sticks.

> *(Led by the* DRUMMER *and*
> TWO SOLDIERS *the* LIEUTENANT
> *makes his way through the
> silent crowd to* HUNT.*)*

Tranquility! Tranquility, friends.

LIEUTENANT: Sir, I have a warrant against you and arrest
you as my prisoner.

HUNT: I willingly surrender myself to any civil
officer who will show me his warrant.

> *(A* CONSTABLE *now pushes
> his way forward)*

CONSTABLE: I will arrest you. I have got information

	upon oath against you.
HUNT:	Then I shall surrender. I shall abide by the Law.
HANNAH:	Do not surrender!
SUSAN:	(shouts) He's got to abide by the Law or they'll hang him.
VOICE:	He hasn't even begun, Lieutenant.
OFFICER:	(shouts order). Cavalry, draw sabres!

> *(The crowd turns and gazes into the distance; the crowd grows fearful and huddles even closer. The crowd hears the bugle sound, the charge, and then the OFFICER's command. The CAVALRY charges the crowd: sound of hoof-beats, neighing of horses, and screaming of people. The crowd screams and panics.)*

HANNAH:	Defend the Orator! They're going to kill him.

> *(HANNAH SMITH pushes forward. SUSAN THISTLEWOOD follows her. The LIEUTENANT is jostled and draws his sword shouting)*

HARRY:	(screaming) Come back, mother. Come back. Get away from here.
LIEUTENANT:	Cut down all who resist you!

> *(The FOOT-SOLDIERS lay about them, shouting)*

FOOT-SOLDIERS:	Have at their flags.

> *(Other FOOT-SOLDIERS rush onto the stage. MEN, WOMEN and*

CHILDREN *are crushed, cut
down, trampled and killed.*

HANNAH: Defend yourselves!
(MRS. THISTLEWOOD *is knocked
unconscious as she screams
and fights to protect the
Orator.* DAVIDSON *picks her up
and carries her away over his
shoulder.* HARRY *runs after
them.* HUNT *stands still.*)

DAVIDSON: Safety! To safety! Harry! Come on, boy.
Come, Hannah.
(*They flee. So does* HANNAH
SMITH. *The chaos subsides.*)

HUNT: There was no need. Murderers. Bloody
Murderers! We were given permission.
(*In the distance the sound of
hoof-beats and the screaming
die away.*
HUNT *is taken off by the
constables.* A WOMAN *raises herself, shouts*)

WOMAN: Lying Murderous Magistrates! Bloody
Sidmouth!
(*Collapses again.*

*Upon the stage, there are the
moans from* MAN, WOMAN *and*
CHILD, *then utter silence.*

Pause.

An ELEGANT OLD MAN *picks his
way, with silver walking stick,
among the dead and dying. He*

*takes out his pince-nez and
surveys the scene.* LORD
SIDMOUTH'S SECRETARY,
HERBERT, *joins him.*
*The two men contemplate
the dead.*)

LORD SIDMOUTH: "Because half a dozen grasshoppers
under a fern make the field ring with
their importunate chink, whilst
thousands of great cattle, reposed
beneath the shadow of the British oak,
chew the cud and are silent, pray do not
imagine that those who make the noise
are the only inhabitants of the field,
that, of course, they are many in number;
or that, after all, they are other than the
little, shrivelled, meagre, hopping, though
loud and troublesome, insects of the
hour".

HERBERT: Burke, my Lord?

LORD SIDMOUTH: (*lighting himself a cheroot*) Yes. Burke.
Liberty, Herbert, if it is to exist at all,
cannot exist without virtue and order.
Liberty must be limited to be possessed.
Though the Revolutionary and the
Christian walk together in this world
they were born at the opposite poles of
the earth, though their physical likeness
is apparent, one is animal ape. (*pause*)
If the Christian is to endure the ape
must perish.

HERBERT: Yourself, my Lord?

LORD SIDMOUTH: (*smiling*) Yes, Sidmouth. (*benignly*)
Herbert, let you and I, who are

LORD SIDMOUTH: accustomed to look with observance at
(contd)   the causes which lead to the fall and
           destruction of nations, give the times
           our most weighty consideration. We
           have seen our country involved in the
           most destructive and arduous contest
           ever recorded in its annals, we have
           witnessed its unexampled and glorious
           struggle, the loyalty and patriotism of
           its people, and finally after more than
           twenty years of war with Bonaparte we
           have beheld our Albion rising victorious,
           towering with renovated fame and
           lustre. Cheering prospects, my dear,
           —in the civilised world we stand supreme
           —and yet, though Rousseau and Paine
           rot in their graves, their evil germs
           rise still. From those two corpses,
           twitches a pestilential flame, which
           if not snuffed out, will rage across
           our island. We must be vigilant, Herbert,
           or that black flame, will bake to plague,
           and roast us.

HERBERT: Indeed it will.

LORD SIDMOUTH: Property is in danger once again. Men, if
           such an exalted name can be given them,
           are traversing this island, intruding them-
           selves into all kinds of society, with
           specious plans for reform in their mouths,
           but with revolution, and plunder in
           their hearts.

HERBERT: They do, my Lord. They are.

LORD SIDMOUTH: Let us not deceive ourselves, we are
           contending for the very body and

LORD SIDMOUTH: substance of our island. Not for the
(contd)   foliage, not for the branches, but
                       for the very trunk of the British Oak.

HERBERT: We must preserve the Oak, my Lord.

LORD SIDMOUTH: We must. I am a Doctor's son and proud
                       of it.

HERBERT: You have a nose for Revolution.

LORD SIDMOUTH: (*smiling*) Traitors, incendiaries, mur-
                       derers, atheists, adulterers, I can smell
                       them all.

HERBERT: Indeed you can.

LORD SIDMOUTH: (*very quietly*) Give the people the vote,
                       Herbert, and they will overwhelm us.
                       (*pause*) Never. (*he grows cheerful again*)
                       Where is Edwards?

HERBERT: In London.

LORD SIDMOUTH: Tell George, I am in the exampling
                       mood (SIDMOUTH *laughs*)

HERBERT: What about Oliver, my Lord? I can
                       highly recommend Oliver.

LORD SIDMOUTH: There is no duty the Executive has to
                       perform, Herbert, so difficult, as putting
                       the right man into the right place. I said;
                       George Edwards!

HERBERT: Yes, my Lord. But with respect George
                       Edwards should not appear himself as
                       witness.

LORD SIDMOUTH: What?

HERBERT: We do not want Government dis-
                       credited.

LORD SIDMOUTH: Quite right.

HERBERT: We do not want another acquittal — as
                       in the case of Castle.

LORD SIDMOUTH: (*interrupting*) You have made your

LORD SIDMOUTH: point. Thank you. Edwards will find a
(contd)   turn-coat on this occasion. He will never
                       himself appear in court.
                              (Pause)
HERBERT: How much am I to offer him?
LORD SIDMOUTH: Be grand, Herbert. Glitter. Tell him to
                       give me the leaders and I will pension
                       him off. Tell him to give me those
                       anarchists, those unbelievers, those
                       men that rejoice over the mangled
                       remains of Princes and Statesmen,
                       such men as butcher Sovereigns — I
                       will hang them. For every one I hang,
                       a hundred acres to Edwards. If we can
                       hang their prophets, we'll rule ten
                       thousand years.
HERBERT: Fifty acres, my Lord?
LORD SIDMOUTH: Never be niggard with a faithful spy.
                       I said a hundred.
HERBERT: Yes, my Lord. Where?
LORD SIDMOUTH: And not in the bogs of Ireland.
HERBERT: South Africa?
LORD SIDMOUTH: Tell him to give me Cobbett and
                       Sir Francis Burdett.
                       For Cobbett, an Estate.
HERBERT: Women also?
LORD SIDMOUTH: They are equal in the sight of God.
                       Women, children? Let's cut 'em off at
                       the cankered root. I know how to use a
                       scalpel.
                              (LORD SIDMOUTH *laughs. The*
                              stage grows darker. LORD
                              SIDMOUTH *moves up-stage)*
                       Back to London, Herbert. I mean surely,

LORD SIDMOUTH: surely Herbert, of all "rights of man",
(contd)   the right of the ignorant man to be
    guided by the wiser, to be gently or
    forcibly, held in the true course, that
    surely, is the indisputablest.

HERBERT: So "Repression" is the order of the day?

LORD SIDMOUTH: It is somewhat more complicated than
    that. Seek to be English. Bad men
    combine the good associate. God bless
    you, Herbert!

HERBERT: God bless you, my Lord.

> (LORD SIDMOUTH *and his*
> SECRETARY HERBERT *leave the*
> *stage. The* LIGHTS *change. Now*
> *the dead and wounded rise and*
> *with the Radicals set up for a*
> *political meeting in the Crown*
> *and Anchor in London.*
>
> SIR FRANCIS BURDETT *takes the*
> *chair.*
>
> SIR FRANCIS *takes off his hat.*)

SIR FRANCIS: Pass my hat for the widows and orphans
    of Manchester. All over England today —
    in Huddersfield, in Leeds, in Bristol,
    and *here* in *London*, the people of our
    land meet in protest. And they meet
    because murder has been committed —
    committed in the most peculiar and
    aggravating circumstances — it has been
    committed under the authority of the
    guardians of the Law — under the
    authority of a Secretary's of State's
    warrant. Silence in this matter, will con-
    stitute an ever open invitation to tyranny.

HANNAH: It will.

DAVIDSON: Did not those Magistrates beguile the people to meet in multitudes and then attack them, and murder indiscriminately men, women and children?

> *(Shouts of "They did".*
> *"They did")*

SIR FRANCIS: In their defence they may hold that the meeting at Manchester was illegal.

SUSAN: If the meeting at St. Peter's Fields was illegal why didn't the Magistrates proclaim it to be so? Why wasn't the Riot Act read before they charged?

HANNAH: *(rising)* I'm a Manchester woman, I heard after, Peter's Field was cleared for cavalry night before!

SIR FRANCIS: I did not know that. The night before!

MABEUF: *(quietly)* Oh this hypocrite Sidmouth. He trusts himself to the timidity of a long injured, patient, suffering starving and exhausted people. My own country, with all its despotic tribunals, will find it hard to match this tyrannical crew.

VERY OLD MAN: I challenge the Spanish Inquisition to match it.

> *(Laughter from some)*

SUSAN: We're not here for laughter! We either shut up and go home or think something serious out.

DAVIDSON: Their victims are placed on record — in my heart I have their victims' names. Ashworth. Ashton. Buckley.

DAVIDSON: Crompton. Fildes. Heys. Jones.
(contd)

VERY OLD MAN: I shall write a hymn of martyrs.
                              (Voice: "Jack Hargreaves too")

TIDD: We need more than a hymn of martyrs.

SUSAN: What I see now is the flashing of a sabre
                    as it goes grinding into a child. Children
                    flying in all directions, their feet slipping
                    in the blood that streamed from their
                    fathers and their mothers; mothers cut
                    down and trampled upon, but still cling-
                    ing to their babies. All that terrible
                    screaming! I'll never forget it. Never.

SIR FRANCIS: As Chairman of this meeting I would like
                    to propose we demand a legal inquiry.

COBBETT: What makes you think they'd give us one?

SUSAN: I would be for an inquiry — but His
                    Royal Highness, has sanctioned, not only
                    sanctioned, but applauded and expressed
                    his *thanks*, to those Magistrates and those
                    Yeomanry. So how can there be an
                    inquiry?

BRUNT: *(standing up)* I'm Butcher Brunt from
                    Cheapside. I'd like to have that bastard
                    Sidmouth's neck under my cleaver. So
                    help me. I say I'm Billy Brunt of
                    Cheapside and I don't care who knows
                    it. I'd cut him in one. Like this.
                              (BRUNT *demonstrates with*
                              both hands)
                    He's a baby murderer — that's what he
                    is! *(pause)* I speak as one who fought
                    at Salamanca with the Duke. I speak
                    as one who's piked and speared and

BRUNT: cut. Who's squared, who's breeched,
(contd)   who's muzzled, who's rounded.
                         (Pause. BRUNT *sits down*
                         then abruptly stands up
                         again)
               And this is the thanks we get for it.
                         *(*BRUNT *sits)*
SIR FRANCIS: Thank you, Mr. Brunt. Yes. Well, what
               I was trying to say was we should all
               go to Westminster and *demand* an
               inquiry. March there and *demand*
               it.
                         (VOICE: *"We should")*
               Now! We can be there in fifteen
               minutes!
                         (Pause)
HANNAH: Buggers would hang us for breakfast if
               we march on Westminster.
SIR FRANCIS: Whether the penalty of that demand
               be death by military execution I know
               not but this I know — a man can
               die but once and never better
               than in vindicating the laws and
               liberties of his country. I am prepared
               to go.
BRUNT: I say chop Sidmouth's the only
               thing that'll do any bloody good.
               I say the whole lot should be
               chopped. The whole government.
               Tower the lot of them. Stick
               their heads on the bloody
               ramparts.
A VOICE: How?
COBBETT: Yes. How? I know, sir, of no enemy of

COBBETT: reform and of the happiness of the country
(contd)   so great as that man . . . or woman . . .
            who would persuade you that we possess
            nothing good, and that all must be torn to
            pieces. There is no principle, no precedent,
            no regulations (except as to mere matter
            of detail), favourable to freedom, which
            is not to be found in the laws of England,
            or in the example of our Ancestors. There-
            fore I say, we may ask for, and we want,
            nothing *new*. We have great constitutional
            laws and principles to which we are
            immoveably attached.

BRUNT: Who says we are?

INGS: Speak for yourself.

COBBETT: I am speaking for myself. We want great
            alterations but we want nothing *new*.

SUSAN: What do you call principles?

COBBETT: Madam, I believe that, as to religion, opinions
            ought to be left as God has made them in our
            minds. I believe that elections ought to be
            free. I believe that the affairs of our nation
            ought to be so managed, that every sober and
            industrious and healthy man may, out of his
            own wages, be able to support himself, wife
            and family in a comfortable and decent
            manner. That the law of nature, as well as the
            law of the land, gives every soul in the com-
            munity a right to a sufficiency of food and
            raiment; and that those who possess the land
            are justly called upon to give good support to
            all, who are unable to labour, or who, being
            able, cannot obtain employment. I believe
            that this support is not a thing given, but a

COBBETT: *right*. I hold, further, that it is the weight of
(contd) taxes, which produces all the miseries this
         nation now suffers. I hold finally that unless
         a great change takes place, and takes place
         speedily, this nation of ours, will become
         feeble and contemptible as well as enslaved;
         and that its capital will be conveyed away to
         enrich and give power to rival nations.

SUSAN: We might believe in your principles but how
         are we going to get a single bloody one of
         them?

COBBETT: I also believe, Madam, and herein seem to lie
         our differences, that it is the duty of us all to
         do our utmost to uphold a government in
         Kings, Lords, and Commons, and that the
         remedy to our miseries consists solely and
         entirely in the reform of the Commons; that
         all good things must be done by a reformed
         Parliament. We must have that first, or we
         shall have nothing good!

SUSAN: You've not answered my questions, have you!
         Mr. Cobbett you have been trying to reform
         Parliament for twenty years. So was I. We
         were married to it! But what I see now is
         oppression. How does one reform that? A
         Reverend Magistrate finds a woman lying at
         the roadside — her naked breasts are gouts of
         blood — when asked what her condition was,
         or whether he did help — he answers smiling
         he did not take particular notice, for she was
         not attractive. I was for the Law but what kind
         of man is that? I ask you again, Cobbett; How
         does one reform oppression?

COBBETT: And I repeat again: With zeal and resolution

COBBETT:
(contd) but by petition.

SUSAN: Petition the rich, that grow in hell. The rich that grow richer, that have within them worms; the rich that puff, and feed on their own vomit. The insatiable rich are not reformable! *Not* reformable. The rich are self perpetuating.

BRUNT: *(angrily)* How do you petition, Lord Sidmouth, but by chopping his bloody head with my cleaver? I done my share at Salamanca: I can use a cleaver. The Duke taught me that.

MABEUF: Forgive me, I am a foreigner. If the law . . . the laws of England are kept . . .

BRUNT: Can't hear you, Frenchy.

MABEUF: *(raising his voice)* If the object of the law is to obtain a great and positive good for the people . . . I mean equal laws, equal rights, and equal justice . . . if your weapons . . . your ammunitions . . . are reason, discussion and persuasion it follows you shall attain your object without anarchy or confusion — my own dear father believed that . . . he too was hanged for His peaceable petitioning . . . that was of course before the invention of the guillotine — but if reason, discussion, etcetera are suppressed by the illegalised mis-government of the country, the exigencies of the time will of necessity suggest such measures as an enlightened and independent people like your own shall think proper to adopt . . . will be compelled to adopt.

BRUNT: I don't understand a word you said, damn my eyes.

MABEUF: Is it not possible that our French Revolution

MABEUF (contd)	was but the precursor of another, and a greater?
DAVIDSON:	Another, and a greater, and a more solemn — which will be the last, and not betrayed.
COBBETT:	The last for whom?
HARRY:	The last for the rich, Mr. Cobbett.
BRUNT:	That's right. The last for the Rich.
SUSAN:	Mr. Cobbett, we have humbly and loyally petitioned for years and years and years. We have got nowhere with petition. Our humility has been rewarded with ruin, with death, and now with murder. We the poor, and the people, have been scorned. Scorned, entirely. It has always been the propertied against the poor. Those who have 'gainst those who've not!
SIR FRANCIS:	That is right, Cobbett. The wealth's all private and the poor do starve.
ADAMS:	We'll never get the vote 'less we take it.
SUSAN:	Now there's only one Law. The rich man's Law. The laws of this land are the chains of the poor.
BRUNT:	Yes. That's the truth of it. I can understand the missis!
INGS:	And *I* can understand her.
TIDD:	And *me!*
SUSAN:	The people of England are no better than slaves. No time to think with the iron wheels on the stones, or the clang, clang, clang of the factory bells that are borne in our babies' ears. The clock has come, the calendar, the watch . . . gone the rhythm of the seasons. But they call us a swinish multitude and do nothing. They send us to

SUSAN: (contd)	work in the dark.
VERY OLD MAN:	Sidmouth holds such poverty is evidence of the wisdom of a divine Providence.
BRUNT:	I say: Chop Sidmouth. I keep sayin' it — don't I?
INGS:	When they passed your hat around for the orphans, Sir Francis. I couldn't put nothing in it because I haven't got a half penny. I who had a butcher's shop in Portsmouth.
ELLEN:	Nor me neither. I haven't got nothing, Mr. Cobbett.
TIDD:	I've got my cobbler's last. That's all I've got.
BRUNT:	Look: I'm Billy Brunt. I say the missis is right. And I don't know her.
COBBETT:	Right or not, friends, don't be inflamed — the cause of freedom *is* making progress.
HARRY:	What progress?
COBBETT:	That progress can only be prevented by our giving way to our passions, by committing acts which admit of no justification in law.
HANNAH:	Don't keep saying Law like bloody parrot. Where the hell's it got us?
COBBETT:	Ladies, I repeat, there's no reform that's good except reform the Government.
ADAMS:	You keep repeating! You're a repeater. *(Laughter)*
SIR FRANCIS:	*(excitedly)* But, Cobbett, what Government! This damned Government of ours is like nothing that ever was heard of before. It's neither a monarchy, an

SIR FRANCIS: aristocracy, nor a democracy. I know no
(contd) name for it. It's a bastard band of nobles
who by sham elections, bribery and corruption have obtained an absolute sway in the
country, having under them for the purposes of show and execution, a wretch
they call a King. They've got a mummery
they call the Church, steel-hearts they call
the Judges, thieves they call the Bank,
savages they call Soldiers and Sailors, and
a set of cackling, wind-bags they call the
House of Commons.

SUSAN: Four years ago this Government of ours
hanged a poor woman in Manchester for
snatching a potato from a cart — then
hanged her starving child that ate it? At
the gallows he cried: "Mother!".

COBBETT: All passion, Madam! You're all passion and
no reason!

MABEUF: But England is famed throughout the
world for its respect of human liberty, and
human life.

SUSAN: I have not finished. Not finished. Not
finished, Mr. Cobbett. Do you understand
me, Mr. Cobbett! I have not finished. Do
you understand, Monsieur, that I have not
even begun? Not begun!

MABEUF: Forgive me I am a foreigner.

SUSAN: Reason! By Christ I say at last we dogs
must bite. Passion! That is all that we are
rich in. I am not deaf, I can hear more than
the rustle of petitions — I hear on the wind
the tears of the poor. I tell you up in
Manchester those soldiers cut our babies!

SUSAN
(contd)

What are you, you Englishmen! Mr. Cobbett, such Englishmen as you are the patientest, most prudent, particular petitioners, the most cowardly wind-bagging hypocritical temporizers in this world.

SIR FRANCIS: That's not fair.

HANNAH: What have we got to lose, Cobbett?

COBBETT: *(furiously)* Everything. *(he turns to* MRS. THISTLEWOOD*)* Madam, the faults that you complain of are just what's best in me! Temporizer! Hypocrite! I who've been to prison for the poor and am beggared for it! What injury, what evil, what destruction, have not this aristocracy and this clergy endeavoured to inflict on me? If I deemed it right — to render evil for evil — right — I should be fully justified in murder! But I do not so deem it. And will never. Power and violence are opposites. As to cowardice. That is a quality universally despised but not universally well defined. By God, Madam, I know you've reason for your grief — when your husband was taken I was sorry for it — but I say again there's no reform that's good except reform the Government that stands. You do not have to tell me, Madam, we are a people robbed and spoiled, snared in our holes and hid in our prison houses. *Who* knows better!

BRUNT: They know it better who are *in* the bloody places.

DRUNKEN
IRISHMAN: *(from the back)* That's right. Free gin.

ADAMS: What about the stink of the gas, and the

ADAMS: (contd)	fuz that renders men old before they're forty?
HARRY:	What about the children deformed and slaughtered by consumption?
COBBETT:	I hear that puffing and blowing and panting and coughing and in my bed at night *I* count the sweating dead.
BRUNT:	But you still sleep in a bed at night don't you, Mr. Cobbett? And beggared or not you've got green fields about your house?
INGS:	There's always meat on your table — ain't there, Cobbett?
COBBETT:	There wasn't in prison.
	(Pause)
ADAMS:	You aren't the only one been to prison, Cobbett.
	(Pause)
DRUNKEN IRISHMAN:	*(from the back)* Got any gin, Cobbett?
VERY OLD MAN:	Let the horseman's scimitars Wheel and flash, like sphereless stars Thirsting to eclipse their burning In a sea of death and mourning.
	(Pause)
COBBETT:	*(quietly and slowly)* Personal accusations . . . or justifications . . . slanders or grievances . . . apart . . . I believe that amongst the virtues of good citizens are fortitude and patience. I don't mean apathy. When a man has to carry on his struggles against corruptions widely rooted he cannot expect the baleful tree to come down at a single blow.
BRUNT:	He can if he has grenades and a taper

BRUNT: to light them with.
(contd)

COBBETT: No, sir, you patiently remove the earth
that props and feeds. The foliage is but the
outward show. The roots are labyrinthine
and I am for going to the roots in politics,
as well as husbandry.

BRUNT: Who'll give Billy Brunt a grenade? I can
show how to throw it.

OLD MAN: It takes a lot of grenades to blow an Oak.

DRUNKEN
IRISHMAN: (*from the back*) Cromwell, would have
hanged the lot of you.
                    (*The* DRUNKEN MAN *gets up and
                    weaves his way to the front*)
You're seditious renegades, and aristocrats.
I am disgusted. It's all treason. And whore-
mong . . . mongers. You don't deserve the
whoresome vote.
                    (*The* DRUNKEN MAN *moves to
                    the door*)
I'm going for a piss.
                    (*Cheers*)

HANNAH: I hope he falls and breaks his bloody neck
on the bloody stairs.
                    (*Laughter*)

SIR FRANCIS: I wonder he didn't piss in here.
                    (*Laughter*)

SUSAN: (*quietly*) So we're back to laughter! You
see what I have come to realise, gentlemen,
is that the time has come when politics is
not enough. While you petition, the poor
will crawl to the workhouse, lie down, and
die with sorrel in their bowels. The only

SUSAN: chance for the poor is Revolution — Revo-
(contd)   lution that must come with a single mighty,
bloody blow. Passion? Violence? I am
beginning to have a lust for it. Law? I say
Necessity has no law. It appears to me that
violence is all that is effective.

SIR FRANCIS: Madam, you dismay me.

COBBETT: Pathetic! Madam. It is pathetic! I suppose
you might be bloody, bold and resolute if
there's ten thousand men would follow you.
I don't believe that such's the case in
England. I doubt that there's two hundred.

HARRY: Someone has to make a start.

ELLEN: Yes and I might go in because I'm poor.

SIR FRANCIS: Mrs. Thistlewood . . . Corruption . . .
government — call it what you will — is
never more delighted than with acts of
violence, and never happier than at the
sight of troops acting against the people.

SUSAN: I am for the night-mare!

DAVIDSON: (shouts) What's absolute has got to be
overthrown.

INGS: Yes: I would rather be a dog that bites than
wait till I've no gums and toothless.

BRUNT: If I'm to be a dog, Mr. Cobbett, I'd like to
get me into the Westminster pit and be dog
Billy, and kill me a hundred rats.

ELLEN: Those who'll be drawn in are those that have
no food.

SUSAN: A week of Revolution will do more for
England than a thousand years of sterile
argument.

MABEUF: Yes! Yes! Revolution! . . . One knows the
Gentlemen of the Right always work

MABEUF: | together . . . that is why they always win.
(contd) | Let us grow. Let us grow! Whether for petition . . . or something . . . more resolute. What is the temper of the country? Who can truly say? The country must be led. The poor must be saved. We shall not solve these problems at a single meeting.
| *(Pause)*
| Can we not at least agree to meet again. Form a Committee. A Committee of the Radicals.

COBBETT: | *(loudly)* What I have noticed, Susie Thistlewood, is that when come to power those who fought for Liberty always deny that Liberty to others, always deny to others those privileges for which themselves they were so resolute.

SUSAN: | How irrelevant, Mr. Cobbett; and in exception — how magnificent to be the first.
| *(A cry is heard from beyond the doors)*

VOICE: | Constables approaching. Constables in the Lane.

SIR FRANCIS: | Out candles.
| *(On stage all blow out their candles: Darkness)*

VOICE: | Alarm. Alarm.

SIR FRANCIS: | Some front. Some back. Some above. Some below.

COBBETT: | Candles with you.

BRUNT: | What! Are we rats?

VERY OLD MAN: | Let us go gently.
| *(There is a scurrying in the*

darkness, then silence)

BRUNT: May the last King be strangled with the guts of the last Priest. Who's got a grenade for a constable!

(*A measured tread is heard upon the stairs; lights approach the doors*)

SIR FRANCIS: Kneel.

(*The doors are thrown open, armed* CONSTABLES *enter the room with torches. Only* DAVIDSON, BRUNT, MABEUF, COBBETT, BURDETT, THE THISTLE-WOODS *and an unknown* POOR MAN *remain. They are kneeling in prayer. The* CONSTABLE RUTHVEN *begins to laugh*)

RUTHVEN: What a nest! On your feet.

(*But the radicals remain in prayer*)

Are you apish Methodists? Are you ranters? I know you all you canting gibberers.

SIR FRANCIS: (*opening his eyes*) Do you now disturb friends in prayer?

RUTHVEN: (*still laughing*) Search these birds for arms and sedition.

(*The* CONSTABLES *begin their search. They call out: "Clean. Clean." When they search* DAVIDSON *they call out: "A Bible". When they come to the* POOR MAN *they draw out a bundle of pamphlets from*

	his shirt and his small clothes, rip another from the lining of his coat, and two more packets are taken from his boots)
RUTHVEN: (contd)	Oh yes. What's your name?
	(*But the* POOR MAN *does not answer. Pause. The* CONSTABLE RUTHVEN *is handed a letter. He reads*)
	Paine's stuff!
THE POOR MAN:	Mr. Paine.
RUTHVEN:	Oh yes? Take him.
SUSAN:	What are you going to do with him?
RUTHVEN:	I don't pass judgement. I'm a bringer-before Magistrates. That's what I am. What's your name, female?
SUSAN:	Thistlewood.
RUTHVEN:	(*to one of his men*) Write it down with your pencil. T . . . H . . . I . . . S . . . T . . . L . . . E . . . W . . . O . . . O . . . D.
	(*The man does so*)
SIR FRANCIS:	Ruthven, I warn you that if there is . . .
RUTHVEN:	Don't you warn *me*, Sir Francis Burdett! I warn *you* there's information on oath against you. (*to* MRS. THISTLEWOOD) You'll make that lad an orphan! Right. Off.
	(*The* CONSTABLES *leave the stage with the* POOR MAN *and the pamphlets. Pause. The Radicals light their candles*)
HARRY:	Will they hang him too?
COBBETT:	Like as not.
SUSAN:	Who is he?

INGS: Who was he?

BRUNT: He'll be at leap-frog.

SUSAN: And we did nothing. We're muck and stones.

TIDD: We are. We're muck!

DAVIDSON: "How long shall the wicked triumph?"

BRUNT: (*passionately*) Damn my eyes. Damn my eyes we're nothing but slaves and cowards.

HARRY: Mr. Cobbett, isn't my Mum right?

COBBETT: (*sadly*) I don't know, boy. I don't know. The Poor will always be divided. Never govern.

> (*The Radicals leave the Crown and Anchor. A drum is heard.* RUTHVEN *and his* CONSTABLES *enter. During* RUTHVEN'S *Proclaimation the conspirators set themselves up in the loft in Cato Street.*)

RUTHVEN: (*The drum beat ceases*) Parliament proclaims a modification and extension of the legislation of 1795 and 1817. My Lord Sidmouth to the people of Albion: The First Act prohibits drilling and military training; the Second Act authorizes Justices to enter and search houses, without warrants, on suspicion of there being arms: the Third Act prohibits meetings exceeding fifty in number with certain exceptions, (County and Parish meetings) and certain additions; the Fourth Act increases the Stamp Duty on periodical publication, raising the cost to sixpence; the Fifth Act extends the powers of the Authorities in judgement of sedition; the Sixth Act extends the powers of The Authorities against libel against the Government. The Government will also

RUTHVEN: mount an assault against the Blasphemous
(contd) Press. (RUTHVEN *looks at the crowd, then at his men*) Right. Off.

> (RUTHVEN *and his men leave the stage.* RUTHVEN *re-echoes the Proclamation.*)

> *(In the Cato Street Loft. BRUNT is sharpening a sword. INGS is hanging sacks over windows. ADAMS is lighting and placing candles. TIDD guards the trap-door and cleans his pistol, MABEUF and HARRY THISTLEWOOD are making grenades by the fixed stove. DAVIDSON is reading. SUSAN THISTLEWOOD sits alone, lost in thought. It is bitterly cold. They sit for a moment listening to the re-echoing of the Six Acts)*

INGS: They must be in the Edgeware Road.
ADAMS: Yes, they're going towards the Park.
MABEUF: Having soldered the tube to the tin case — form of a barrel — put in three ounces and a half of gunpowder.

> (MABEUF *weighs the gunpowder on a pair of scales and does so*)

HARRY: What's the priming?
MABEUF: Saltpetre, powder and brimstone. Pitch the tin, wrap round it with rope yarn, and cement that with rosin and tar.
ADAMS: It's bloody cold up here.

INGS: (*raising a gin bottle*) Here's to you. Mabeuf.

MABEUF: (*raising his bottle*) Here's to us all.

ADAMS: (*raising his bottle*)

BRUNT: (*raising his bottle*)

TIDD: (*raising his bottle*)

BRUNT: Yes, thank you, damn my eyes though I never liked foreigners and fought against your countrymen many times.

INGS: (*to* MABEUF) Brunt's never liked Froggies.

DAVIDSON: Such barriers must be broken down. My father's Attorney General in Kingston, Mabeuf, Kingston, West Indies. But my black mother was the making of me.
Now she is gone and buried and I am the lesser for it, By Christ.

ADAMS: It's our mothers that have made all of us.

BRUNT: (*to* MABEUF) Without you we'd be nothing in this business and I thank you for it.

TIDD: (*drinking*)

INGS: (*eating*)

MABEUF: It is *my* mother we have to thank for all this. La Comtesse. Dieu Merci. (*pause*) I too loved my mother.

ADAMS: Susie, I do not say I am clever with the sword but I can use the sword sufficient.

SUSAN: Listen. I think aloud. It rests upon ourselves. If only the first blow can be struck. Say at the Tower, at the Bank, at Parliament or the Monarchy. Spitalfields, the Minories and Smithfield will rise, the Country Places will sweep all before them.

INGS: The shoemakers are ready.

ADAMS: And the weavers.

SUSAN: I say we need a single act! An act of such

SUSAN: significance the poor will raise their heads like
(contd)   wolves and rush into the streets and bite.

TIDD: We should recruit the Regent's Canal Navigators, Susie. They're a handy lot.

INGS: And the Paddington Canal, Susie.

SUSAN: It is *we* ourselves alone must do it.

MABEUF: Yes, London is the heart of the matter.

DAVIDSON: London is the Paris of the Albion.

SUSAN: Come. Let us think.

(Pause. They do so)

INGS: (sadly) It was Cobbett that put us down at
that meeting.

HARRY: If Cobbett was in we'd be further on now.

SUSAN: Don't say that, Harry!

HARRY: I have read of many Revolutions, mother,
but none that has succeeded without the co-
operation of some great men and I do not
think there are any to aid the present proceed-
ings.

DAVIDSON: Yes by the very nature of their poverty the
poor are always the most cowardly class.

SUSAN: (irritated) That's just what I said isn't it! We
must do it outselves. *We* must be great.

(Fause)

BRUNT: (angrily) It *was* Cobbett that put us down at
that meeting! Damn my eyes if he were to come
into this loft now I would run him through,
murder him and take care after I had done it,
it should never be found out. If we do nothing
else we must murder Sidmouth and Cobbett.

TIDD: All the middle men should go. They always
hold you back the furthest. (pause) I was one
of those myself.

HARRY: Cobbett'll die in his bed.

(Pause)

ADAMS: *(to* DAVIDSON *)* I'll bet your weapon is bigger than Cobbett's by a foot.

DAVIDSON: It is.

ADAMS: And I believe Miss Salt of Litchfield can testify to that.

DAVIDSON: *(laughing)* She screamed with joy when first she saw it, then called for her mother to help.

BRUNT: To lift it I suppose!

ADAMS: *(laughing)* No to put Salt upon it.

SUSAN: What to catch it by the tail?

> *(Unexpectedly* SUSAN THISTLE-WOOD *too breaks into a peal of laughter)*

ADAMS: How did that father do when he saw it?

DAVIDSON: Shot at it with his pistol.

BRUNT: Why did he come to miss?

DAVIDSON: To tell the truth the bullet went through my hat.

ADAMS: You were wearing your hat?

SUSAN: *(sardonically)* He always keeps on his hat with minors.

TIDD: How old was she?

DAVIDSON: Sixteen at that time.

BRUNT: You like them young then?

DAVIDSON: I like them tender. Sunday school mistresses and choir girls is my heart's desire. Though you Susie are now my favourite age. *(pause)* But I did love Miss Salt. I was young then. *(once again he shrieks with laughter)* I was besalted!

ADAMS: *(smiling)* Yes, he was besalted.

DAVIDSON: Love is a disease you know, dear Robert.

ADAMS: It is. I have a friend I treasure. He was with

ADAMS: me in the Blues. He's in a Public House in
(contd)   Camberwell. The Donkey. He did me good
          service once with a Constable. This Constable
          was circumcised. He was a Jew they say. But
          others said Irish.
                              (*Pause*)
SUSAN: (*quietly*) If any one of you feel fear in passing
          through the shadow of death . . . in spite of
          your oaths . . . in spite of your declarations
          . . . I hereby release you. (*pause*) Now is the
          time to go.
                              (*Pause*)
MABEUF: I think we are all determined.
ALL: We are, Susie.
HARRY: We are all determined, mum.
BRUNT: It will do nothing dodging on it, Susie.
MABEUF: If a major centre is captured all will spread.
INGS: If the flame is lit. *If!*
SUSAN: Precisely.
TIDD: They all have arms.
BRUNT: The Scots will only advance when they see a
          rocket.
TIDD: Yes they always need a rocket, those Scots.
MABEUF: Suppose . . .
SUSAN: Yes?
MABEUF: The Ministers are said to be going to a fête
          given by the Spanish Ambassador.
HARRY: All of them?
MABEUF: So I understand.
SUSAN: When?
MABEUF: Soon. I read so.
HARRY: Where?
MABEUF: I don't know.
ADAMS: The New Times.

MABEUF: Was it?

TIDD: It was. It was in the New Times.

SUSAN: When?

MABEUF: What?

SUSAN: When are they meeting? In the snow? A fête
          in the winter! Besides the innocent would
          perish with the guilty. I'll not have that.
                    (*Pause*)

HARRY: With these grenades how long does the ex-
          plosion take from the lighting of the fuse?

MABEUF: Half a minute?

HARRY: That can be a very long time.

BRUNT: It can.

HARRY: A lot could go wrong in half a minute.

BRUNT: It can.
                    (*Pause*)
          It does.

ADAMS: Some of the Ministers are often in the Park.
          Castlereagh in particular. My mother and I
          have seen him there several times. Castle-
          reagh's always going with whores. Canning
          has a vice or two but Sidmouth keeps to him-
          self at Broadstairs.

SUSAN: We need more than an assassination or a mur-
          der. I tell you what we need's an act.

MABEUF: You are right.
                    (*Long pause*)

TIDD: (*passionately*) I wish to do something for my
          friends. The truth is most of them are
          starving. My daughter's a good girl but she
          hasn't had a decent bed in nine month —
          that's why she's whoring and diseased in
          Spitalfields. No I have never murdered a man
          but now I am prepared to do so. (*pause*)

TIDD: Speaking of cobbing I am also a shoe-maker,
(contd)   Mabeuf. If your boots need mending, give
               'em to me.

MABEUF: Merci.

TIDD: I have frequently expressed to my wife the
               thought that I will die upon the gallows. She
               is distressed at my entertaining this idea but
               I know the fate assigned me well enough.

MABEUF: Don't say that.

TIDD: Oh yes. (*pause*) I dream it every month. Some-
               times twice or three times.
                             (*Long pause*)

INGS: (*angrily*) We must let them know in the
               Prisons. I have a sister in Newgate with a six
               months' baby and nothing to lie on but a mat.
               She was thrown there for selling one of
               Paine's addresses. (*pause*) She's all spirit,
               my Mary, and no matter. Her husband's name
               is Swann. The paper wrote that she was "an
               abandoned creature" — but that's not so
               neither. One of her poems ended: "Now,
               now, or never can your chain be broke;
               Swift then rise and give the fatal stroke". But
               I am afraid whatever we accomplish it will be
               too late for my sister, Mary.

BRUNT: Is your money all gone?

INGS: Gone. If you cannot support your family the
               only thing for it is to become an anti-
               Christian and a Deist and come to London.

DAVIDSON: No, no I cannot agree to that. There is no
               logic to that.

INGS: Such has been my miserable experience.
                             (*Pause*)

BRUNT: (*to* INGS) Whenever you think of your

BRUNT: (contd)	children you go down at the mouth.
INGS:	I do. I never forget my children. (*Pause*) Yes she's very brave, my sister, Mary.
SUSAN:	What does she call her baby?
INGS:	I don't know. I don't know.

(Pause)

ADAMS:	I too have to do something good before I die.
TIDD:	It's a long walk to Portsmouth. I was there once. In the old days I went into Church and prayed but all that got me nowhere. I've never seen a thin Bishop.
ADAMS:	I've known Bishops.
HARRY:	When we are in power we must have new medals.
BRUNT:	I've got medals. Salamanca. Vitoria. It was hot down there. But very cold in the winter. I never suffered more from cold. We had beer and onion for breakfast. All the men farting like horses. You couldn't drink the water. Looked like an army of chimney sweeps. The night before the battle there was a thunderstorm. Some soldiers were blinded. Some were smothered in tents when the horses ran off. After the light was what you might call pearly. In the dawn. The Frenchies made a mistake. They come up too quick on the left. The Duke saw that. Went through the gap and we caught 'em. That night I slept where I was — with a wall of dead Frenchies around me — to keep out that cutting wind.
MABEUF:	How they have rewarded you.
BRUNT:	Yes. Unlike you all I never got on with my mother. Or my wife: I have done better with

BRUNT: whores than either of those women. (*pause*)
(contd) Whores have been good to me. I have an invention for preventing horses coming upon a crowd. It is a machine with four wheels with sharp scythes which will mow down attacking yeoman and cavalry. I thought to use that in Spain. I sent a letter to the Duke. He was very kind in his acknowledgement — but I never heard further. I've got nothing against the Duke. Of course that was not the place to use it, Susie.

SUSAN: No.

TIDD: We should have used it at Manchester.

SUSAN: Yes.

BRUNT: Yes, we should have.

(*Pause*)

HARRY: Is the explosion from these grenades great destruction?

BRUNT: In small rooms very great?

ADAMS: Another friend of mine I treasure is a smithy.

DAVIDSON: (*pacing about*) Your French Revolution, Mabeuf, has shown us that if a thing is bad, the longer it has done harm the worse, and the sooner it's abolished, the better.

HARRY: That's right.

DAVIDSON: Mabeuf, your Revolution shows that resolute men can reverse the verdict of History. Shows that men of consequence can throw off the dead weight of status quo and prejudice; of tradition. By Christ and Jesus, whom I so adore, I say, all hereditary government is in its nature tyranny.

INGS: Though I am a deist I drink to that.

(INGS *does so*)

DAVIDSON: Cobbett speaks for all men . . . of any property — Paine speaks, I speak, Jesu speaks . . .
for all men.

(Pause)

SUSAN: *(to* INGS*)* When we have our plan we will make
it known to every prison in London.

DAVIDSON: *(getting excited)* All the land, the waters,
the mines, the houses, and all permanent
feudal property must return to the people,
the whole people, to be administered in
partnership by the parishes.

MABEUF: Sovereignty to the people.

DAVIDSON: Yes. To the People. To the People. To the
People.

(Pause)

INGS: Oh my Christ if only we could have it.

DAVIDSON: As the power is always on the side of the
people when they choose to act, it follows as
a matter of course that whenever a single
point is put to the test of the sword the
people are always ultimately victorious.

TIDD: Would to God it were so!

ADAMS: I fear it's not.

INGS: No. It's not. It's not!

HARRY: It isn't

BRUNT: Somehow or other we must do it. We must
do something!

SUSAN: But we have no plan! We have no plan!

> *(Pause. There is a knocking
> at the trapdoor in the stage.
> All take up weapons.* MABEUF
> *thrusts a pistol into the boy's
> hand)*

ADAMS: B. U. T.

HANNAH: *(from below)* T. O. N.
                             (ADAMS *raises the trap-door.*
                             HANNAH SMITH *enters the loft,*
                             still covered in snow)
               Cold night.
ADAMS: Mabeuf has bought us gin.
                             (ADAMS *passes his flask.*
                             HANNAH SMITH *drinks*)
HANNAH: *(drinking)* Liberty or Death.
SUSAN: How are you, my love?
HANNAH: In this world there's not enough that's
               resolute. If man's prepared to die it's easy . . .
               if not . . . bugger it!
SUSAN: What's the bad news?
HANNAH: Its bloody cold. They're all bloody cold.
               They're all bloody freezing, fucking, cold.
TIDD: In the spring time they might do it.
BRUNT: In the summer heat, damn my eyes, they'll
               do it.
ADAMS: Summer is coming. In the summer evenings I
               know how to get a pound or two from an
               officer.
HANNAH: How are you, son?
HARRY: Well.
HANNAH: How many have you made?
HARRY: *(holding up a grenade)* Fifty-seven.
DAVIDSON: Yes. If none feared death it were easy!
TIDD: Every other English face is small poxed —
               every other child is dead before he's five.
SUSAN: So any good news?
HANNAH: Susie, I went to Fox Court, Hole in the Wall
               Passage, Brook's Market. They're not in the
               mood for a rising, Susie. Not in the temper for
               it. Cobbett has left London. Burdett's writing!

TIDD: What about the Navigators?

HANNAH: They're going back to work.

INGS: And the shoe-makers?

HANNAH: That strike too is broken.

HARRY: The truth is there's nobody but us.

SUSAN: (*irritated*) Haven't I been saying that? Did
            you get any news from the North?

HANNAH: The usual resolutions — nothing to lift us.
            They have cowed them.

SUSAN: Oh Arthur, Arthur, come back down and
            help us.

                        (*pause*)

            I'm down at the mouth, Hannah, I cannot
            think what to do.

DAVIDSON: Have a drink of gin, my love.

ADAMS: Yes. (*to* HANNAH) Were you followed?

HANNAH: No, by Christ.

SUSAN: What do you take her for?

HANNAH: I'd run any through that followed.

ADAMS: I only ask because I'm good at that myself.
            At following. Officers and such-like. Gentle-
            men.

                        (*Pause*)

INGS: If it weren't for the potato we'd have had the
            Revolution long ago.

MABEUF: I envy the young. They will see something
            worth looking at.

HANNAH: Wilson's taken.

TIDD: What for?

HANNAH: Arson.

MABEUF: Who informed?

HANNAH: Oliver.

SUSAN: *We* must light the tinder! The only instrument
            is sitting here. (*she goes and picks up one of the*

SUSAN: *grenades*) We are the Committee of the Revo-
(contd)   lution; think of these, my friends, as the fruits
             of the earth — where are we going to plant
             them? Perish if it must be all of us providing
             we do something good with one of these!
                          (*Pause*)
BRUNT: Put it in Sidmouth's letter box.
SUSAN: I keep telling you, Billy, that would light no
             spark. The act must have some size to it. A
             little act will turn the mob against us. We
             must have grandeur.
DAVIDSON: She's right by God. There's no time nor
             money for aught else. Without the thunder
             you cannot have the rain.
SUSAN: How do we toll the bell? How do we put the
             smell of blood into their starving noses?
DAVIDSON: How do we bring the rain that cleanses?
                       (*Long pause*)
SUSAN: Oh Jesus I can't think any more!
HARRY: Mum: I'm cold.
SUSAN: I'll come and warm you.
                        (SUSAN THISTLEWOOD *comes
                        and sits beside her son, bring-
                        ing a candle with her and
                        placing it beside them*)
SUSAN: Come into my arms.
HARRY: (*snuggles up beside her*) Mum, it's no good
             just doing something stupid and getting
             caught and hanged.
SUSAN: I know that, my love.
HARRY: That wouldn't do any good. They'd forget
             us in a week. No-one remembers, Dad.
SUSAN: I do.
HARRY: You know what I mean.

SUSAN: Yes.

HARRY: Tell me what it was like.

SUSAN: What?

HARRY: When they hanged him.

SUSAN: No.

HARRY: I've the right.

SUSAN: No.

HARRY: Mum, you tell me.

SUSAN: No.

HARRY: Mum, I have to know it. Go on.

SUSAN: No.

HARRY: Go on.

SUSAN: No! No! No! I'll not!

> (*There is a pause then* SUSAN
> THISTLEWOOD *gives a huge cry
> of grief*)

Arthur! Arthur!

> (*Long pause*)

HARRY: What were his last words?

SUSAN: Nothing. He didn't say nothing.

> (*Pause*)

HARRY: Can I have a drop of that gin, Mum?

> (SUSAN THISTLEWOOD *passes
> her mug*)

Do I look like him?

SUSAN: Very much. (*Pause*) Harry, maybe we should
give up and go back to the country. I could
find something, surely. If people won't come
together and help themselves what's the
point? I could go into service.

HARRY: Father once said . . . if only there was some
way . . . some way he could kill all of them
. . . all the Ministers. Not just Sidmouth
but all of them at once. (*pause*) Would

that be grand enough?

SUSAN: What?

HARRY: All of them at once. That's what Father said.

        (*Long pause*)

SUSAN: (*to all*) Did you hear that?

BRUNT: Yes and damn my eyes I believe that would.

DAVIDSON: That would be a text for everything.

SUSAN: Yes. (*pause*) But how? Poor man *he* never solved it.

MABEUF: *We* have to solve it.

BRUNT: Put grenades into their carriages.

SUSAN: All at once! How do you murder all of His Majesty's Ministers at once? How do you murder the whole of the British Cabinet?

HANNAH: I see no way of it.

MABEUF: There must be a way!

        (*Pause*)

SUSAN: Hannah's right. I propose we all split up and take what paths we can. As your leader I have to tell you honestly we've come to nothing. But that's better than the gallows and nothing done. That's nothing for nothing!

MABEUF: At least we wait until my fifty pounds is gone.

BRUNT: All this gin and these grenades are wasted, Susie?

TIDD: We've hired this loft for nothing.

INGS: Don't say it, Susie.

ADAMS: Something must turn up.

BRUNT: The very least we can do is murder Sidmouth.

SUSAN: That will accomplish nothing — I've told you that again and again and again and again.

        (*Pause*)

INGS: Should we all go to America?

BRUNT: No. We've got to do something here. We was

BRUNT: born for it. We was born here. Not in
(contd)   America! We're not bloody fucking
            Americans. We're got to do something here,
            right here, right up here, right up here in
            this bloody loft in Cato Street, we've got
            to start somethin' up here!

SUSAN: Let's put it to the vote. I am for the break up.

BRUNT: Damn my eyes I say we've got to use up
            Mabeuf's fifty pounds on something up here!

MABEUF: We've got to.

SUSAN: Yes? Willy? Hannah? Tidd? Adams? Ings?
            Harry? Monsieur?

                        (*Long pause. The* STAGE GOES
                        DARK *except for the light that
                        falls on* MONSIEUR MABEUF — *in
                        this light* MABEUF *walks down
                        stage to a corner where* LORD
                        SIDMOUTH, *the Home Secretary,
                        sits on his chair*)

LORD
SIDMOUTH: Good evening, George.

                        (*THE CURTAIN FALLS*)

ACT TWO

LORD SIDMOUTH *and* MABEUF *sit
smoking cheroots.* MABEUF *now speaks
without his French accent.*

LORD SIDMOUTH:*(raising his pince-nez)* Robert Adams:
Yes, in the summer, he used to get
money in Hyde Park. Let me look. Yes:
(he glances at some papers) Last demand
four months ago from a gentleman in St.
James' Street.

MABEUF: Anyone I know?

LORD SIDMOUTH:*(laughing)* I don't know who you know,
do I George? A Baronet. Ten pound he
had off him. Caught him by the collar
and accused him.

MABEUF: Of an unnatural offence?

LORD SIDMOUTH:Yes. Poor gentleman. *(pause)* A cousin
of my wife's. Yes. Adams had a witness
with him, of course. Wright — a black-
smith; Clapham. The whole family,
Adams have a history. It says here, this
Robert, is given to painting up and
clothing himself as a female. In Black-
friars.

MABEUF: I thought as much.

LORD SIDMOUTH:An interesting patient! At the hour of
seven. When the bells chime. Ding dong.
Ding dong.
(They laugh)

LORD SIDMOUTH:It's very good to see you, George.

MABEUF: Mutual, my Lord.

LORD SIDMOUTH:They are desperate you say?

MABEUF: Very low.

LORD SIDMOUTH: What vipers!

> *(Pause)*

MABEUF: How is your wife?

LORD SIDMOUTH: Don't speak of her!

MABEUF: I won't then.

LORD SIDMOUTH: The domestic burden is enormous. Got just like her mother. Yes. Monstrous woman.

> *(Pause)*

Is there quality in any of these wretches?

MABEUF: Men are so simple aren't they?

LORD SIDMOUTH: Oh indeed he who seeks to deceive will find many who will allow it. It is necessary to understand that side of mankind. Did they question you greatly?

MABEUF: Not enough. They're too intent upon their miseries. Or purposes rather. Will you hang them *all*?

LORD SIDMOUTH: Miseries?

MABEUF: Well, you know what I mean, my Lord.

LORD SIDMOUTH: I hope you're *not* getting sentimental.

> *(Pause)*

So do you think we can draw in Cobbett, or Burdett, etcetera?

MABEUF: None of the centre men.

LORD SIDMOUTH: Is there no way?

MABEUF: *I* do not know it.

LORD SIDMOUTH: That disappoints me.

MABEUF: Not as much as myself! *(they laugh)* I'll be fortunate to get a garden!

LORD SIDMOUTH: I shall be generous.

MABEUF: My Lord, you can make such an
               example of these wretches as will
               put all such others down for twenty
               years.

LORD SIDMOUTH: *(sharply)* I am an authority on show
               and precept. You can have a hundred
               acres. Where? South Africa?

MABEUF: God forbid! America.

LORD SIDMOUTH: You should do well there - I can
               arrange that. Philadelphia? Maryland?

MABEUF: Boston, my Lord.

LORD SIDMOUTH: Boston. Take an Irish name.

MABEUF: Yes.

                    (MABEUF rises)
               What would you have done, my Lord,
               if I'd put this in your pocket?

LORD SIDMOUTH: What, George?

                    (MABEUF produces a grenade.)
               Is it real?

MABEUF: I can light it.

LORD SIDMOUTH: I fear you're getting sentimental. The
               woman?

MABEUF: *(laughs sardonically)* No. Were I the
               leader . . . *(he pauses)* were I committed
               otherwise I should . . .

LORD SIDMOUTH: Yes, George?

MABEUF: Nothing, my Lord.
                    (Pause)

LORD SIDMOUTH: Nothing?

MABEUF: Nothing?
                    (Pause)
               So Mrs. Edwards will enter . . . and
               then the officers. Two minutes?

LORD SIDMOUTH:Three minutes. (*he laughs*) The officers
will enter on the hour of seven.

MABEUF: Thank you.

LORD SIDMOUTH:Ding dong, George.

> (SIDMOUTH *blows his silver
> whistle.* HERBERT *enters*)

Give him his newspaper and Tommy.

HERBERT: Yes, my Lord.

> (HERBERT *gives* MABEUF *a
> newspaper and a little dog.*)

MABEUF: Goodnight.

> (MABEUF *goes.*)

HERBERT: Will you have a brandy?

LORD SIDMOUTH:Something in those wretches seems to
have touched him. I am wondering . . .
I think everyone should go to the
country for the week. Do you know
what I mean?

HERBERT: Of course, my Lord.

LORD SIDMOUTH:(*smiling*) Sometimes one has a presenti-
ment. I'll take her Ladyship to Broad-
stairs. What is *her* mood?

HERBERT: Dreadful;

LORD SIDMOUTH:I *will* have a brandy. What did he say
that fellow was called?

HERBERT: Walters. Harold Walters. Shall you come
with me when I make the invitation?

LORD SIDMOUTH:(*sardonically*) Yes, I'd like to see George's
wife. A large brandy, Herbert. And warm
it. Yes, to know the man you have to
know the wife. What a lovely little
dog that Tommy is. (*very seriously*)
Herbert, you'll keep your wits about
you.

HERBERT: My Lord?

LORD SIDMOUTH: When . . . Never think the hour *cannot* come.

HERBERT: The hour?

LORD SIDMOUTH: When all is ripe. Out of a clear blue sky, Herbert. Should that moment come, Herbert, light the grenade yourself.

HERBERT: (*smiling*) You are a realist.

LORD SIDMOUTH: God bless you, Herbert.

> (*The lights fade — they go up again on the Cato Street Loft*)

ADAMS: What else can I say!

DAVIDSON: Nothing!

ADAMS: It was the gin!

BRUNT: The Duke would bring out the drums and the muskets.

INGS: And line him up.

HARRY: Can't fire a musket in here.

TIDD: Billy, they'll catch it in the Edgware Road. We aren't a hundred yards from Marble Arch, Billy.

ADAMS: So much for friendship.

HANNAH: Babies.

BRUNT: Got to have discipline.

INGS: Somebody's got to cut him then.

BRUNT: I'll cut him.

INGS: I'll cut him.

ADAMS: I'll scream.

BRUNT: (*raising his knife*) So you'll scream a little. They won't hear that in the Arch.

TIDD: There's neighbours you know. That milk-man'll be up. And that ostler.

SUSAN: Put down your knives, you two.

BRUNT: Damn my eyes, Missis, sentry is sentry.

SUSAN: Put your knives in your belts you bloody
            fools. We're all to blame. What's the time
            now?

HARRY: I've heard eight strike.

SUSAN: How long's he been gone. That's the point.

TIDD: Don't know what time he slipped out do
            we.

SUSAN: I mean how long is it since we missed him?

HANNAH: He could've been gone all night.

                    (Pause)

BRUNT: It might be he put something in that gin.

INGS: He could've poisoned us.

ADAMS: *(sarcastically)* What makes you think he
            didn't, Brunt?

BRUNT: I always said I never liked Frenchies.

ADAMS: So much for friendship.

                    (Pause)

DAVIDSON: If he'd been coming back with Constables
            they'd have been up the ladder now.

TIDD: Yes it don't take long to rouse up
            Constables and the Military.

                    (Pause)

ADAMS: *(looking at* BRUNT *and* INGS*)* I say again:
            so much for friendship!

BRUNT: I have a headache.

ADAMS: So you should have.

SUSAN: We all got drunk.

BRUNT: It was *his* gin.

DAVIDSON: They might be waiting downstairs for us to split.

BRUNT: Damn my eyes so they might?

INGS: Yes and seize us as we descend the ladder.

*(HARRY THISTLEWOOD goes to
the trap-door - puts his ear to
it. Silence)*

HARRY: I can't hear anything.

ADAMS: You wouldn't would you.

SUSAN: Look out of the window again.

*(HARRY THISTLEWOOD and
DAVIDSON do so)*

HARRY: Nothing stirring on the roofs.

ADAMS: There wouldn't be would there.

SUSAN: What kind of light is it out there?

HARRY: It's a dark morning.

TIDD: If they want to they can starve us out.

DAVIDSON: Yes. They can.

(Pause)

Some can go out the window.

HANNAH: Believe we'd have heard something.

HARRY: I'll go down the ladder, Mum. If I'm not back in five minutes you'll know something's wrong.

ADAMS: Suppose some Constable puts a knife to your throat and makes you call the password.

HARRY: *(Quietly)* I'll not call it.

SUSAN: I'll go.

HANNAH: No, lad's best.

SUSAN: All right. Get your guns, your swords and your grenades ready. Gather round the trap so anyone comes up, but Harry, gets it.

ADAMS: I'm not turning my back on those two mad men.

SUSAN: Robert, you come beside me and Hannah.

ADAMS: I will.

(ADAMS does do.)

SUSAN: All right. Into position. Billy, you'll lift the trap for Harry.

> *(The* CONSPIRATORS *take their positions round the trap-door* ADAMS *still eyeing* BRUNT *and* INGS, HANNAH SMITH *picking up a grenade and holding a candle beside the fuse when there is heard a tapping at the trap-door and a cheerful cry from* MABEUF *from below B. U. T.) Silence on the stage. Then again B. U. T.*

BRUNT: Let the bastard up.

SUSAN: Don't know who's with him.

> *(Pause)*

All right. We'll let him up.

> *(* SUSAN THISTLEWOOD *moves to the trap)*

Ings, you lift at the side. Billy if it's him that comes through you pin him. If it isn't him, Willy, you thrust with the sword.

> *(Once again from below* MABEUF *shouts B. U. T. This time* SUSAN THISTLEWOOD *calls in answer:* T. O. N. INGS *raises the trap-door and* MABEUF *enters the loft carrying the dog* TOMMY *with a newspaper in his jacket pocket.* BRUNT *goes to seize* MABEUF *but stops at the sight*

of the dog. INGS *drops the*
trap-door. Silence)

MABEUF: *(resuming his French accent)* Whatever's the
          matter friends?
                    (Pause)
          You think I have betrayed you. Oh mon
          Dieu. I went to fetch my dog. Didn't you tell
          our General, Billy? I shake you, I whisper to
          you. "When our General wakes I say tell her I
          have gone to get my little dog". *(Pause)*
          Billy, I whisper to you in the night I am
          worried. "I have forgot my little dog." Here,
          Tommy, say "hello" to my friends.

HANNAH: He is a lovely little dog.

SUSAN: Why didn't you wake me?

MABEUF: You were dreaming. I heard you whisper:
          "Arthur," and I left you.

HANNAH: Looks frightened.

MABEUF: He's always been uneasy with strangers.

ADAMS: What was I doing?

MABEUF: You were sleeping by the fire.

ADAMS: It's true I did wake by the stove.

MABEUF: I don't know why you don't remember,
          Billy. You said: "Adios."

BRUNT: I did? *(pause)* I must have been asleep.

INGS: When you thought he was awake he must
          have been asleep.

TIDD: He must have been dreaming - that's
          Spanish: "Adios."

MABEUF: Yes. That must be it. But his eyes were open.
          Would you like to hold my dog "Tommy", Hannah?

HANNAH: I would.

                    (HANNAH SMITH *takes the dog*

and suddenly DAVIDSON *starts*
to laugh and laugh and laugh)

TIDD: All that worry over nothing!

ADAMS: Over a little dog.

(Others laugh)

SUSAN: Alright. But from now on no-one goes in or out of this loft without my permission. Sleeping or not. Tiddy, you go on guard.

TIDD: Right, Missis.

HANNAH: Fed him?

MABEUF: Of course. He hadn't had nothing for two days. I swear by God he cried tears when he saw me.

DAVIDSON: Is that a newspaper?

MABEUF: The New Times.

DAVIDSON: Can I read it?

MABEUF: Oh yes.

*(*MABEUF *hands over the newspaper)*

SUSAN: Harry, make us all some tea.

*(*HARRY THISTLEWOOD *goes to the stove)*

ADAMS: I might have been killed on account of that little dog. Such is life.

SUSAN: From now on we trust no-one but ourselves.

ADAMS: I agree with that.

(Pause)

TIDD: They tell me anyone can get into the House of Commons with an order - well no-one would think anything of one of us going in there with a book - in the hollow we put one of our old pistol barrels, cut into pieces about three or four inches long, plugged

TIDD: up each end with lead, and the centre filled
(contd)   with powder and a touch-hole. Half a
         dozen such books could be made for half
         a dozen of us. Then we could go in when
         the House is full — we could go into the
         Gallery and throw them at Sidmouth and
         the Cabinet Bench.

BRUNT: Damn my eyes.

INGS: (*very excited*) Yes. Yes! One of us might
         have a bottle of phosphorous, and a lighted
         match might be taken with a piece of rope
         without giving any alarm to the persons
         present and applied to the fuse - which
         would communicate with the contents of
         your cases and then light, light, light, and
         throw, throw, throw.

ADAMS: What a destruction that would make.

BRUNT: We'd have our men at the door.

SUSAN: But we could not be sure who was in the
         House. Or not.

BRUNT: No. Those lazy bastards.

SUSAN: Nor if there's any there we would wish to
         spare.

TIDD: They say the Horse Guards will be down at
         Windsor on the King's funeral.

ADAMS: If we could get the two pieces of cannon in
         Gray's Inn Lane and the six pieces in the
         Artillery ground we would have possession
         of London before morning.

SUSAN: Possession of London!

ADAMS: When the news should reach Windsor the
         soldiers would be so tired from being
         up all night as to be incapable.

SUSAN: Incapable of what?

ADAMS: Returning to London.

SUSAN: So tired! Are you a military man? Have you never heard of such a thing as a bivouac?

ADAMS: Maybe we could seize the sea-ports.

SUSAN: You're an idiot!

BRUNT: What about the Mansion House?

SUSAN: What about the Mansion House!

BRUNT: Occupy it.

SUSAN: Our entire Committee would lose itself in the Mansion House. We might as well go wandering through the Tower of Babel. How is that to do with anything and what is that to murdering the Cabinet? If we cannot think of anything better I say we split. Bloody fools!

HANNAH: Suppose . . .

SUSAN: Yes?

HANNAH: No good. No, it's no good is it, little Tommy.

SUSAN: Never mind about little Tommy. Think!

TIDD: You were right, Missis, when you said it's no good getting hanged for nothing. But I shall go to my own hanging. I dreamed it again last night.

INGS: That was the gin.

TIDD: Gin or not I dreamed it.

SUSAN: Let everybody sit quiet till the tea's strong and think.

(Long pause)

BRUNT: Damn my eyes I'll do something or other. I'll burn a house or two. I must do something.

INGS: I can't go back to Portsmouth having done nothing.

DAVIDSON: Sir William Draper Best is to be married.

SUSAN: Put down that bloody newspaper and think,
            Willy!
DAVIDSON: There was a cousin of his who came to Litch-
            field to stay with the Bishop.
SUSAN: Oh Jesus are we now to have the Society
            news!
HANNAH: Suppose . . .
SUSAN: Yes.
HANNAH: No good.
DAVIDSON: By God! By Christ! I have it. Here it is be-
            fore our very eyes. Here in the New Times!

> (DAVIDSON*paces excitedly up
> and down waving the copy of
> the New Times*)

SUSAN: What is in the New Times?
DAVIDSON: They are meeting all together.
SUSAN: Who are?
DAVIDSON: The Cabinet! All of them. They are having a
            dinner at Lord Harrowby's in Grosvenor
            Square.

> (*Pause*)

SUSAN: When?
DAVIDSON: (*looking at the newspaper*) Tonight. All of
            them! The twenty-third. Wednesday. What's
            today?

> (*Pause*)

MABEUF: Wednesday. Wednesday the twenty-third.
BRUNT: Till now have I disbelieved in the existence of
            God - now I am well satisfied.
DAVIDSON: This Dinner is appointed by God.
SUSAN: (*calmly*) We go to the door with a note to
            present to the Earl of Harrowby; when the
            door is open we will rush in directly, seize the
            servants, present a pistol to them and directly

SUSAN:
(contd)

threaten them with death if they offer the least resistance or noise.

BRUNT:

This done, a party will rush forward to take command of the stairs. One man is to fire arms and he will be well protected by another holding a grenade; two will take the head of the stairs leading to the lower part of the house. If any servants attempt to make a retreat these men with the hand grenades are to clap fire to them, and flight them in amongst them.

INGS:

All these objects are for the securing of the house.

TIDD:

And those men who are to go in for the assassination, are to rush in directly after.

HANNAH:

I will go in then.

(Pause)

SUSAN:

Yes, the women will go in then.

DAVIDSON:

I must see the women at that!

INGS:

(jumping up and down) I will enter the room first, I will go in with a brace of pistols, a cutlass, and a knife in my pocket, and after the two swordsmen have despatched them I will cut every head off that is in that room and Lord Castlereagh's head and Lord Sidmouth's head I will bring away in a bag. For this purpose I will provide two bags. As soon as I get into the room I shall say, "Well my Lords. I have as good men here as at Manchester Yeomanry. Enter citizens and do your duty".

DAVIDSON:

By God we shall make History. Tiger, tiger, burning bright.

BRUNT:

We will get those to throw fire-balls into the straw at all the Barracks. That will stifle man

BRUNT: and beast. My friend Cook will capture the
(contd)   cannon. Then the Bank of England. All
           London will burn. I have many friends. This
           will spark everyone. This will get them in the
           streets. The Navigators will come down from
           the canals.

SUSAN: At any rate the plan is reasonable - first
           things first. Details later. Planned and precise.

MABEUF: We must get some men of substance.
                    (*He glances at* SUSAN THISTLE-
                    WOOD)
           Men for show. Names that will raise names.

HANNAH: And women!

MABEUF: And women. *Now* we might get Burdett and
           Cobbett. Cartwright, Shuttleworth and
           Taylor. Yes Cobbett might come for this!

SUSAN: Rot Cobbett! We'll do it outselves. Cobbett
           and Burdett would never do it. What time is
           the dinner?

DAVIDSON: (*looking at the newspaper*) Eight.

SUSAN: From now on - no-one moves without an
           order. We must have secrecy. No-ones leaves
           my sight. Only *we* must know the business.

INGS: I feel myself very faint.

DAVIDSON: What is the manifesto?

SUSAN: Yes draw it up, Willy. Your tyrants are
           destroyed. The friends of liberty are now
           called upon to come forward. The provisional
           Government is now sitting. Mrs. Thistlewood,
           Secretary, 23rd February, 1820;
                    (*Pause*)

SUSAN: No gin, no beer! Cool heads are necessary,
           for this day's work.

TIDD: Yes, till the business - no gin.

SUSAN:	Till the business is done.
ADAMS:	We had enough gin last night didn't we!
SUSAN:	All right, Robert. All right!
BRUNT:	Their blood'll be our gin.
MABEUF:	(*laughing*) Home made gin!
BRUNT:	By God we will do it. It will be known as the West End job.
INGS:	We will write out our manifesto on cartridge paper.

(Silence)

	Damn my eyes I must not forget my steel. I will procure Castlereagh's hands also. They will be thought a great deal of in future days.
TIDD:	You cannot keep still for thinking of it.
INGS:	I can't. I can't.
SUSAN:	If only Arthur had lived!
DAVIDSON:	There is a Heaven and he looks down upon us.
SUSAN:	We can do all that we want with twenty men. I can get them easy. They must not be told the business till the last.
MABEUF:	Good. Good.
SUSAN:	*They* shall drink but we stay sober.
INGS:	Yes *they* can have the rest of the gin.
BRUNT:	Right. That'll fire 'em. They'll be ready for anything on gin.
SUSAN:	Right. I'll be back at six! On the hour precisely.

(MRS. THISTLEWOOD leaves
the loft.
The LIGHTS FADE.)
(Early evening in the loft.
DAVIDSON is writing his

manifesto on cartridge paper.
ADAMS *is on guard.* TIDD, BRUNT,
and INGS *are preparing the*
weapons. MABEUF *is cooking*
at the stove).

DAVIDSON: Declaration of Independence. Citizens:
Since your Government was manifestly cor-
rupt we have overthrown it with fire and
sword.

BRUNT: The tyrants already are destroyed.

INGS: The whole land will be bathed in blood.
Listen I have to have a drop of gin. I have
to.

(INGS *takes a drink*)

DAVIDSON: Citizens: Let us not decide to imitate. Let us
begin to create the whole man. Let us go forward night and day, in the company of men,
in the company of all men.

TIDD: What a party!

DAVIDSON: It is not a question of a return to nature. It is
a question of restoring the dignity of man.
The privacy of man. It is a question of des-
troying the rhythm that mutilates. Citizens,
the tyrants have made us into monstrosities.
Citizens, brothers, together we will climb out
of the abyss. Citizens, unite! There are
miracles. And here is such a one. At last the
soul of man may soar on earth into the light
of day.

BRUNT: And say "Murder your brother if he's not
with you in all this business."

DAVIDSON: "Scots wha hae wi Wallace bled
Scots that Bruce has often led
Welcome to your gory bed

DAVIDSON: Death or Victory."
(contd)   Come out of your holes you horde or
                rats, bite out their eyes, gnaw them to
                pieces. Rise up oh abased horde. Restore
                yourselves.

>   (DAVIDSON *starts to dance*
>   HANNAH *joins him.*)

HANNAH: *(sings)* Scots wha hae wi Wallace bled etc.

>   (*The others join in.*
>   *Once again there is a banging*
>   *at the trapdoor. Silence.* SUSAN
>   THISTLEWOOD *below calls.*
>   "B.U.T." ADAMS *answers.* "T.O.N."
>   *and raises the trap-door.* SUSAN
>   THISTLEWOOD *enters, followed*
>   *by* ELLEN COX, PALIN, GILCHRIST,
>   LORD WILKINSON - *the* VERY OLD
>   MAN, *and various others*)

MABEUF: Welcome. Welcome, friends.
BRUNT: There's stew, and cheese, and bread and gin.
DAVIDSON: *(grinning)* The Lord helps those that help
                themselves.
INGS: Eat, and drink and examine friends.
BRUNT: Cheese and gin. Gin friends, Gin!

>   (*The poor gather ravenously*
>   *around the food*)

SUSAN: Proceed, Mabeuf.
MABEUF: Here is our arsenal, friends. Harry.

>   (MABEUF *and* HARRY THISTLE-
>   WOOD *tip open the sacks of*
>   *arms onto the bed*)

GILCHRIST: But what are we to do?
SUSAN: Wait till all are gathered then ask again.
BRUNT: It is called the West End job.

MABEUF:	Pikes, grenades - muskets, broad-swords, pistols, blunder-busses - ball cartridges, gun-powder.
VERY OLD MAN:	Magnificent.

(The poor crowd round and take up various weapons)

PALIN:	I like the feel of this.
GILCHRIST:	This sword is sharp and balanced.
ELLEN:	And this is light enough for my using.
GILCHRIST:	*(dressed very poorly)* Let me have the rapier.
VERY OLD MAN:	I got it first.
PALIN:	But what's the business?
SUSAN:	Patience. The house is near.
MABEUF:	Drink, friends. Gin is here.
BRUNT:	Yes. Have a drop of gin to warm you.
INGS:	*(demonstrating)* This is my knife. I have twisted around the handle a quantity of thread - in order that when satuated with the blood of our victims it might not slip out of my hand.
GILCHRIST:	*(drinking)* Is that a Butcher's knife?
BRUNT:	*(laughing)* It is a Butcher's knife for he's a Butcher.

(Pause)

GILCHRIST:	It is want of food which brought me here. Death - death would be a pleasure to me - I would sooner be hanged this instant, than turned into the street there; for I should not know where to get a bit of bread for my family; and if I had fifty necks, I'd rather have them all broken one after the other than see my children starve.

MABEUF:	You may take a loaf with you.
GILCHRIST:	But I have no means to get to any place.
SUSAN:	You can walk it.
MABEUF:	Yes, you can walk where you are going.
PALIN:	When do we leave?
SUSAN:	On the hour.
VERY OLD MAN:	What hour?
SUSAN:	The hour of seven. The hour of liberty.
DAVIDSON:	The hour of Liberty, friends. The hour of the flowing of the soul. We are your Provisional Government. This is your Cabinet of Ministers. We shall rule.
PALIN:	Rule?
INGS:	A flowing of the soul! At seven o.clock!
BRUNT:	A letting and a leeching, damn my eyes. That's at eight.
DAVIDSON:	Behold we stand at the door and knock.
GILCHRIST:	*(eating)* What door is that?
PALIN:	But what is to be done?
SUSAN:	Such opportunity friends can never be, must never be, will not be, lost.
HARRY:	*(holding up a grenade)* Friends, one of these has been known to kill twelve persons.
DAVIDSON:	Two makes twenty four.
MABEUF:	And we have fifty nine of them.
SUSAN:	Once accomplished other consequences will follow.
BRUNT:	*(laughing)* You know the larger body is already gone ahead to arrange matters; we the smaller are left to do the business.
INGS:	Once we have done it there will be a crowd about the door - but our escape is taken care of by the larger body.

SUSAN: Yes once the first blow is struck, friends, we will be joined by immense numbers.

DAVIDSON: A host. Drink up, dear friends.

PALIN: But what is the first blow and what is the business?

INGS: *(passionately)* Rather than give up the business I will go to the house myself alone and blow it up, though I perish myself in the ruins, for all can see we have got that with which we can easily do it. Who are you to deny me?

GILCHRIST: I am nobody.

HARRY: *(to GILCHRIST)* Put yourself under mother's command. And you will be somebody.

SUSAN: *(cheerfully)* I have two ideas: violence and liberty. The minority must abide by the majority decision. One step above the sublime makes the ridiculous - one step above the ridiculous makes the sublime again.

ELLEN: *(eating)* But where is the neighbourhood and what is the door?

BRUNT: Missis, we will draw lots and whoever the fellow is upon whom the lot falls shall be one of those that do it.

PALIN: I draw no lots.

SUSAN: No, I want volunteers. Raise your hands.
(They do so)

DAVIDSON: All hands are up but this man's.
(Slowly PALIN raises his hand)

BRUNT: If a man should attempt it and not succeed he is a good man but if he shows any cowardice he deserves to be run through the body.

PALIN: In part or whole what have we volunteered for?

SUSAN:	It is not the hour of seven. At the hour of seven the plan shall be revealed. You are going to light a fire, dear friends, a conflagration that will rage through England. You are going to ascend from hell with a grenade in each fist.
DAVIDSON:	You are going to be reborn.
SUSAN:	You are going to murder.
MAN:	Murder?
SUSAN:	*(inspired)* Murder! Murder committed of the people, by the people, for the people. Murder organized and murder taught. Murder led, and murder applied. We, the murderers are the key to the door of liberty. We the murderers will forge and bind a nation.
DAVIDSON:	*(excited)* You will recover your innocence, dear friends. Murder for justice, murder for purity, murder for freedom.
SUSAN:	*(quietly)* Murder. Murder. Murder. Murder. You are the executioners.
MAN:	I am for it.
ELLEN:	So am I by Christ!
OTHER VOICES:	"And I", "And I". We are the Executioners of Justice.
DAVIDSON:	Into the healing fire, out of the abyss, into the cleansing waters, drink from the blood of the lamb.
PALIN:	But what I want to know is who's to be murdered and where?

(Pause)

And when?

(Pause)

PALIN: And first. And why?

       (Long pause)

SUSAN: Make an example of him. I cannot have a mistake.

       (Slowly ADAMS *raises his sword.* PALIN *backs* BRUNT *and* INGS *move behind him and raise their sword-points into* PALIN's *back)*

INGS: I'll do it.

MABEUF: The General has to do it.

       (MABEUF *throws his sword to* SUSAN THISTLEWOOD. MABEUF *laughs.* SUSAN THISTLEWOOD *catches the sword. Pause. Another loud knocking is heard and a man's voice calls B.U.T. And fainter a woman also. Pause)*

SUSAN: Quiet.

       (Again the cries are heard)

       Hannah?

HANNAH: None of mine.

HARRY: Nor mine.

SUSAN: Monsieur.

MABEUF: I have not been out.

       (Long pause)

SUSAN: *(to* ADAMS *)* Answer.

ADAMS: T. O. N.

       (ADAMS *raises the trap. After a moment a poor man,* WALTERS, *enters, holding a baby in his arms, followed by* MRS. GEORGE EDWARDS *and her daughter* MARY *)*

SUSAN:	*(calmly)* Who are you? *(Pause)* What is your business?
WALTERS:	We were told there was to be a party. Eating and drinking. He told us to be here at seven.
MRS. EDWARDS:	Eating and drinking.
WALTERS:	Amongst friends.
SUSAN:	Who's friends?
MRS. EDWARDS:	I don't know.
WALTERS:	Just an evening amongst friends.
MRS. EDWARDS:	Two gentlemen called.
WALTERS:	In top hats.
MRS. EDWARDS:	One old: one young.

MABEUF:	*(to* MRS. EDWARDS*)* Welcome, my dear. Welcome to our party. Mr. Walters, how enchanting to meet you. Let me hold the little baby. Emily, welcome. Mary, my darling, don't be frightened. Don't you remember your father?
	          (Slowly the little girl goes to
	          MABEUF. MABEUF *kisses her*
	          and the baby)

MARY:	When are you coming home, daddy?
MABEUF:	Eat, Mr. Walters, drink.
SUSAN:	These are yours, Monsieur?
MABEUF:	*(laughing)* Not the bastard. That is Mrs. Edwards and Mr. Walters.
MARY:	When are you coming home, Daddy? *(Pause)*
SUSAN:	*(screams)* Kill him!
MABEUF:	*(reverting to his English voice)* One moment. Do I hear the chimes?

(All over London the bells chime seven. Pause)

MABEUF:
(Contd.)
Yes. Seven o'clock!

MRS. EDWARDS: Why do you call him, Monsieur?

MABEUF: Here, Willy, Catch! Bless you.

(MABEUF throws the baby to MRS. THISTLEWOOD, jumps down the trap, and is gone)

SUSAN: After him. After him. Kill him. kill him.

(SUSAN THISTLEWOOD runs to the trap-door, followed by BRUNT, and HANNAH SMITH, but now whistles are blown and shouting is heard and military orders are uttered and RUTHVEN the Constable comes up through the trap. All draw back - including SUSAN THISTLEWOOD)

RUTHVEN: Why what a nest is here. What a pretty nest!

(SMITHERS enters)

SMITHERS: Lay down your arms.

(Pause. With a scream of horror and rage SUSAN THISTLE— WOOD shoots Constable SMITHERS)

(falling) Oh Lord. Oh my God I am . . .

(SMITHERS dies)

SUSAN: *(screams)* Kill the bastards! Throw them down the stairs. Jump out of the windows. Away! Away! Away!

(SUSAN THISTLEWOOD throws herself at RUTHVEN. There is

*panic, commotion fighting
and hysteria. Several shots are
fired from several pistols.*
SOLDIERS *enter the loft. The
candles are all out and there
is total darkness. Then the only
sounds that can be heard are
the crying of* MRS. EDWARD's
*baby and the barking of the
dog, Tommy)*

A COURT

The JUSTICES *take their seats.*

CHIEF JUSTICE: Robert Adams.
(ADAMS *rises and bows)*
Robert Adams, you have the thanks of a
grateful country. Since you have turned
King's evidence your pardon is entire.

ADAMS: I would like to say I am sorry about
Susie Thistlewood and the others. I am
not sorry about Brunt and Ings. But I am
sorry my mother is shamed. When I look
at the world I sometimes wonder if it
wasn't God that was thrown out of
Heaven and that the Devil is now sitting
up there on his yellow throne.

CHIEF JUSTICE: Leave the Court, Adams.

ADAMS: Thank you, my Lord. Thank you for
keeping your bargain and sparing me. I
shall go back to Clapham to my mother.
But I shall not go back to my trade in
the park.
(ADAMS *bows and leaves)*

*(The prisoners are double-
ironed:* SUSAN THISTLEWOOD,
HARRY THISTLEWOOD, HANNAH
SMITH, BRUNT, INGS, MRS. EDWARDS,
MARY EDWARDS, TIDD, DAVIDSON,
GILCHRIST, WALTERS, LORD
WILKINSON, *and* ELLEN COX)

CHIEF JUSTICE: The Gentlemen of the Jury have been dis-
(Contd)   missed with the thanks of our Country.
             There are those of your accomplices yet
             to be apprehended - comfort yourselves
             that they are sure to be so.
             (Pause)
             Mrs. Edwards, Mary Edwards, you are
             released. Strike off their irons.
             (The CONSTABLE *does so)*

MRS. EDWARDS: *(looking at her lover)* But what about
             Walters!

CHIEF JUSTICE: Mr. Walters will remain seated.

MRS. EDWARDS: Where's my baby?

CHIEF JUSTICE: I have no knowledge of that. *(pause)*

MRS. EDWARDS: *(dazed)* But Walters has done nothing.

CHIEF JUSTICE: Leave the Court.
             (Mrs. EDWARDS *and her
             daughter do so)*
             Susan Thistlewood, Harry Thistlewood,
             Hannah Smith, Thomas Brunt, James
             Ings, Richard Tidd, William Davidson,
             Harold Walters, Joseph Gilchrist, Ellen
             Cox and Lord Wilkinson, you stand
             convicted upon the third count of the
             indictment - namely that you did com-
             pass, imagine and invent to levy war
             against the King, and that you did

assemble, meet, conspire, consult to devise, arrange, and mature plans, in order by force and constraint to compel our Lord the King to change his measures and his counsels. What have you to say why you should not receive judgement to die according to the Law?

(Pause)

Mrs. Thistlewood, since you seem to have been in all things the leader, shall you speak first?

(SUSAN THISTLEWOOD rises)

SUSAN: I am asked, my Lords, what I have to say that judgement of death should not be passed on me according to the law. This to me is mockery - You, sirs, are Lords - yes you are privileged traitors to our country - because you *lord* it over the lives and property of the sovereign people. The judges of this country, who have heretofore been considered the counsel of the accused, are now without exception, in all cases between the Crown and the People, the most implacable enemies of the latter.

WALTERS: *(rises and shouts)* I was told. A gentleman told me "An evening amongst friends". Two gentlemen came and told me that.

CHIEF JUSTICE: Your turn will come, Walters.

WALTERS: Oh God.

SUSAN: *(looking at Walters)* However . . . yes however. . . as to finer things . . . as to motives . . . as to the immorality of our projects . . . the assassination of tyrants

SUSAN: now seems to me to be completely justified.
(contd)   When any man, or set of men, place them-
            selves above the laws of their country, there
            is no other means of bringing them to justice
            but through the arm of a private individual.
            If the laws of the community are not strong
            enough to prevent such tyrants from murder-
            ing the community, it becomes the duty of
            every member of the community to rid his
            country of its oppressors. For while there is
            treason against the State, or treason against
            the Sovereign, there is also treason against
            the People. England is still in the chains of
            slavery — I quit it without regret — I shall
            soon be consigned to the grave — my body
            will be put beneath the soil whereon I first
            drew breath. Let the night wind blow over
            me.
                          (SUSAN THISTLEWOOD *sits
                          down then rises abruptly)*
            Take this down, Gentlemen of the Press:
            For life as it respects myself, I care not, the
            form the etiquette of a trial has been gone
            through, and condemned me, but the time
            will come, and with vengeance, when the
            Blood of the Slain will be the people's
            watchword, and Insurrection a public duty.
            I prophesy that! I further say . . . upon
            consideration . . . yes upon serious con-
            sideration . . . that I was a fool! What we
            should have done — and with stealth and
            cunning — was to have perfected assassin-
            ation. We should have co-ordinated private
            murders — all over this land — should have

SUSAN:
(contd)

formed a league of murderers. Tyrants
are to be murdered! Their wives and
their children. Alone and privately. In
the dark. They must be taken unawares
with knife and grenade. They must not
be allowed to sleep! There must not be
a single moment they do not fear the
shadow at the window, the step upon
the path, the creaking of the lock.
Disperse, record my words, begin, and
do it! Go out about like Christ's dis-
ciples — spread my Gospel.

CHIEF JUSTICE: William Davidson.

DAVIDSON:

(rises) Oh we will be avenged. That day
will come. I am only sorry I did not
have the chance to complete my manifesto. I have many children. To them I
say avenge your poor black father. Or
grand-father. Or great grand-father.

                (DAVIDSON *laughs etcetera*)

CHIEF JUSTICE: James Ings.

INGS:

I have very little to say. My abilities
will not allow me to speak. For Adams
I care nothing. I should have killed him.
I do not mind dying if you will let
Edwards come forward and die with me
on the scaffold. If I was going to
assassinate the Ministers, I do not see
that it is so bad as starvation, in my
opinion, my Lord. Or going back to die
in Portsmouth with nothing for my wife
and children. All Constables, Magistrates
and false Judges should be murdered.
And Ministers.

CHIEF JUSTICE: William Thomas Brunt.

BRUNT: I had intended to have written the observations which I should make but have not had the benefit of ink and paper. I am a man of my word and not a shuttlecock. Mabeuf, and Adams have betrayed us. That's it. I am not a man who would have stopped. Oh no, I would have gone through with it to the very bottom. With pleasure will I die as a martyr in Liberty's cause. Though afterward you may quarter my body. I will mount the scaffold with a smile. I am only sorry we failed in the business. I am only sorry we were such fools as to be taken in by a Frenchman. I never liked foreigners. Or Spaniards. Yes, we should have split up.

         (BRUNT *sits then rises abruptly*)

Lord Sidmouth's a clever bastard.

CHIEF JUSTICE: Hannah Smith.

HANNAH: The only good thing about George Edwards was his little dog and that fooled me. As for you, my Lord, rot you.

CHIEF JUSTICE: Ellen Cox.

ELLEN: My Lord they are all false witnesses.

CHIEF JUSTICE: Lord Wilkinson.

VERY OLD MAN: Insatiable curiosity.

CHIEF JUSTICE: What?

VERY OLD MAN: These fine pains are for my curiosity.

         (The VERY OLD MAN *sits down)*

CHIEF JUSTICE: Richard Tidd.

TIDD: It is just as I predicted.

CHIEF JUSTICE: Walters.

WALTERS:　　　　Edwards has done me over his wife.
　　　　　　　　　(WALTERS bursts into tears)
CHIEF JUSTICE:　Gilchrist.
　　　　　　　　　(GILCHRIST too bursts into tears)

GILCHRIST:　　　I appeal to God who now hears me and
knows that it is true I went into the
room at Cato Street because I saw men
and women and children going up there
who told me there was food for nothing.
And there were men and women and
children there eating bread and cheese
which they cut with a sword. I cut some
for myself. That is how I had the sword
and this was all I knew of the business
and yet I stand here convicted of high
treason. I have served my King and
Country faithfully for twelve years, and
this is my recompense. This is my
recompense O God!
　　　　　　　　　(GILCHRIST sobs again)

CHIEF JUSTICE:　Harry Thistlewood.
HARRY:　　　　There is no evidence to convict me
of high treason but I have no objection
to die.

CHIEF JUSTICE:　Mrs. Thistlewood has complained that
the Court has refused to hear testimony
of some witnesses that would impugn
the name of Adams. But the case did not
depend upon the evidence of Adams alone.
Some of you have thought fit to say much
on the character of a person - Edwards
or Mabeuf - who has not appeared in the
Court. I do not know if such a person

CHIEF JUSTICE: exists. The Court can proceed only on
(Contd) the evidence brought before it. Upon
the testimony however, which has been
adduced against you, there was evidence
abundant to induce a Jury of your
countrymen to come to a conclusion that
all of you have taken an active part in
the crimes imputed in the indictment.
Your intention, to have steeped your
hands in the blood of fourteen persons,
persons to many of you unknown, is
without precedent in England. Yes,
this crime of assassination in mass is
hitherto a stranger to our country, and
after your melancholy example, it will
again I hope become unknown amongst
us. Before I pass the awful sentence of
the law upon you, I exhort you, I implore
you, to employ the time left to you in
this life, to endeavour by prayer to obtain
mercy from that Almighty Power before
whom you will shortly appear. Humility
and contrition! Seek mercy through
your blessed Redeemer.

>*(The* LORD CHIEF JUSTICE *now*
>*puts on his black velvet cap)*

Susan Thistlewood, Thomas Brunt,
James . . .

>*(But now one of the other*
>JUSTICES *takes the* LORD CHIEF
>JUSTICE's *arm and whispers*
>*in his ear.*
>*Pause)*

Oh yes.

(The LORD CHIEF JUSTICE *consults a paper)*

CHIEF JUSTICE: (Contd)
Lord Wilkinson, in view of your changing your plea from Not Guilty, to Guilty, your sentence is commuted by the person of the Sovereign to transportation for life. Mr. Walters, Mr. Gilchrist, Ellen Cox, Harry Thistlewood - you also will be transported.

VERY OLD MAN:
Oh my Lord. Thank you, my Lord. Thank you.

(Pause)

To where. Australia?

CHIEF JUSTICE:
To New South Wales.

VERY OLD MAN:
Oh my Lord! Might they take off my irons? Enormous weight, my Lord. Immense.

CHIEF JUSTICE:
I am sure the gaoler will grant you every indulgence consistent with his safety. Leave the Court, Lord Wilkinson.

(The VERY OLD MAN *is taken from the Court)*

HARRY:
I do not want to be transported.

CHIEF JUSTICE:
Take him from the Court.

HARRY:
I won't go. I won't. I want to die with my mother and my father.

SUSAN:
Go, my love. Go.

DAVIDSON:
Avenge us, Harry.

SUSAN:
Begin again, my love.

CHIEF JUSTICE:
I said: Take him from the Court.

(Struggling and weeping the boy is taken out)

HARRY:
(screaming back to his mother) I love you, mum. I loved you!

(COX, WALTERS and GILCHRIST
are taken out. The CHIEF
JUSTICE glances at the other
JUSTICES. They nod. The LORD
CHIEF JUSTICE puts back his
velvet cap)

CHIEF JUSTICE: *(reading)* Susan Thistlewood, Hannah
Smith, Thomas Brunt, Richard Tidd,
James Ings, William Davidson, the sentence of the law is that you, and each of
you, be taken from hence to the goal
from whence you came and from thence
you shall be drawn upon a hurdle to a
place of execution, and be there hanged
by the neck until you be dead; and that
afterwards your heads shall be severed
from your bodies, and your bodies be
divided into four quarters, to be disposed
of as his Majesty thinks fit. And may
God in his infinite goodness have mercy
on your souls.

THE CRIER: *(loudly)* Amen.

THE JUSTICES: Amen.

(The JUSTICES take up their
Bench and chairs and leave the
stage; the CONSTABLES shep-
herd their prisoners to the
gallows.

SUSAN: Keep your spirits - all will soon be well.
(The CONSTABLES start to take
off the prisoners' irons. The
PRISONERS shake hands and
cry to each other "God bless
you". And, "Good to see you

again." "Did you sleep heartily"? The prisoners hands are pinioned behind their backs; the REVEREND MR. COTTON *reads the burial service, commencing at the words: "I am the Resurrection and the Life" etc.* INGS *is laughing.* DAVIDSON *prays devoutly. The prisoners stop at the foot of the scaffold. Silence. A bell sounds. The crowd begins to gather both in the audience and on the stage. Silence. Then the bell tolls again. A hooded* EXECUTIONER *mounts the platform of the scaffold. After a moment the* REVEREND MR. COTTON *joins this* "DOCTOR")

DOCTOR: Mrs. Thistlewood.

(SUSAN THISTLEWOOD *ascends the platform. The* DOCTOR *arranges one of the ropes around her neck)*

REV. COTTON: Tell me the subject of your thoughts on the hereafter.

SUSAN: Have you the orange you promised me?

REV. COTTON: Yes.

SUSAN: Give me a piece of it.

(The REVEREND MR. COTTON *gives* SUSAN THISTLEWOOD *a piece of an orange —* SUSAN THISTLEWOOD *raises her pinioned hands and sucks it)*

SUSAN: (contd)	My religion is the religion of humanity, Reverend. My country is the world and my religion is to do good.
VOICE:	God Almighty bless you!
SUSAN:	*(smiling)* Is that you, Adams? Is that you, Edwards? Is that you, Mabeuf?
REV. COTTON:	No, no.
VOICES:	God Almighty bless you, Susan. It's none of them.
BRUNT:	Adams is in the Park with a mouse-trap up his arse-hole waiting for a Minister of the Crown.
SUSAN:	*(She looks down at the rest of the prisoners)* Come up and join me, sweethearts.
BRUNT:	Aye to be sure.
INGS:	*(sings out)* Oh give me death or liberty. *(BRUNT and INGS ascend, laughing)*
DOCTOR:	Mr. Tidd. *(TIDD trembles and moans)*
TIDD:	It is just as I predicted.
BRUNT:	Come up my old cock-o-wax.
TIDD:	*(weeping)* I always said it would be so. I said it.
INGS:	Keep up your spirits, Tiddy. Come up — the air is fresh.
SUSAN:	It all will be over soon, dear Richard. *(TIDD starts to run up the steps, stumbles, falls back, recovers himself, and rushes on-to the platform of the scaffold. The crowd cheers. The DOCTOR puts the rope round TIDD's neck)*

BRUNT: Three cheers for Mr. Tidd, Hip, hip.
>*(The crowd cheers "Hooray")*

Hip, hip,
>*(The crowd cheers "Hooray")*

Hip, hip,
>*(The crowd cheers "Hooray")*

REV. COTTON: Miss Smith.

HANNAH: Mrs. Smith.
>*(HANNAH SMITH ascends, calling to the DOCTOR)*

HANNAH: I want knot on right - not on left side.
>*(The DOCTOR adjusts the noose as requested)*

Thank you, Doctor. Pain of dying will be diminished by change.
>*(To the REVEREND MR. COTTON)*

Give me bit of Susie's orange.
>*(The REVEREND does so)*

DAVIDSON: *(below)* Oh Redeemer. Redeemer! Intervene.
>*(DAVIDSON begins to shake)*

Save us. Not in pity but because we would have done better for our country than what they have. In the name of wisdom, save us.

SUSAN: Come up, Willy, for Christ's sake.

TIDD: *(screams to the REVEREND MR. COTTON)* Remember me to King George the Fourth. God bless him and may he have a long reign. I left a jacket behind in the cell - will you give it to my wife?

REV. COTTON: I will.
>*(Pause)*

INGS: *(desperately)* My little dear boy, William Stone Ings, I hope you will live . . . to hear . . . when the remains of your poor father are mouldered to dust. I hope you will make a bright man in society. The road you ought to pursue is to be honest, sober, industrious and upright in all your dealings; and to do unto all men as you would they should do unto you. My dear boy put your trust in one God . . . Kiss your mother, your sisters.

SUSAN: *(shouting cheerfully)* These are the gallows they always use but the coffins for us I suppose are new.

BRUNT: Life's but a jest and all things show it; I thought so once but now I know it. Eh, Susie?

(The crowd cheer)

I fought with the Duke at Salamanca!

DAVIDSON: Kiss me on the lips, Reverend. Yours is the last kiss but one.

(The REVEREND MR. COTTON *does so)*

Susan!

SUSAN: *(shouts)* What?

DAVIDSON: I love you.

SUSAN: Come up, Willy!

DOCTOR: Come up, Mr. Davidson.

INGS: *(screams)* Come up for Christ's sake and get it over with.

*(*DAVIDSON *rises and ascends)*

DOCTOR: *(to* COTTON*)* Ready.

SUSAN: Tie the handkerchiefs tight over all our eyes.

INGS: *(shouts)* No handkerchiefs!
                   (The crowd takes up the cry.
                   "No handkerchiefs")
SUSAN: *(quietly)* No handkerchiefs.
DAVIDSON: Hold my hand, Reverend.
REV. COTTON: I cannot?
DAVIDSON: Why cannot?
BRUNT: *(laughing)* Because when the trap falls
                   he'll go with you.
                   (The LIEUTENANT *shouts*
                   "Because when the trap falls
                   he'd go with you!")
INGS: *(weeping)* I think the most beautiful
                   thing in this world, was to lie on one's
                   back in a green garden, looking up at the
                   skylight in the sky, through the branches
                   of a large tree.
                   (Pause)
BRUNT: Outside Portsmouth.
INGS: Yes.
REV. COTTON: Then shall the dust return to the earth as
                   it was, and the spirit to God that gave it.
INGS: *(screams)* I wish that my spirit might be
                   conveyed to the King, and that his
                   Majesty or his cooks make turtle-soup of
                   it.
                   (BRUNT *laughs)*
HANNAH: *(screams)* I suppose if I had not lost my
                   children through starvation I would
                   never have been so foolish over that
                   little dog.
SUSAN: *(shouts)* Why don't you come up and
                   cut us down?
                   (Pause)

SUSAN: *(screams)* I say by Christ let those
(Contd)   amongst you that have pluck come up
                    and cut us down. Where there is no
                    vision the people perish. One generation
                    passeth away and another generation
                    cometh. Do you not identify at all with
                    us, my friends? Are we strangers to you?
                    Are we all animals and beasts? Will you
                    remember us?

> *(Silence. Then the trap falls.
> And after a while the bodies
> swing. The crowd groans as
> the bodies swing. Then the
> bodies are still. Slowly the
> crowd melts away - the* REV.
> MR. COTTON *sits there with his
> bible. The* DOCTOR *looks into
> the trap. Silence. Darkness
> falls.* LORD SIDMOUTH *enters.*
> HERBERT *enters with him hold-
> ing a torch.* GEORGE EDWARDS
> *stands alone - a remnant of the
> crowd.)*

HERBERT: Mr. Edwards.

LORD SIDMOUTH: George.

EDWARDS: Were *you* in the crowd, my lord?

HERBERT: No. He had other business.

LORD SIDMOUTH: Was there a moment when you wavered,
                    George?

> *(* EDWARDS *laughs)*

HERBERT: Couldn't afford to - could he?

EDWARDS: Revolutions are not made out of rose-
                    water are they?

LORD SIDMOUTH: No.

EDWARDS: Spontaneity has to be organised and
                  guided.
                            (*Pause*)
                  They were never in touch.
                            (*Pause*)
LORD SIDMOUTH:Someone's still living.
EDWARDS: Still living? Yes.
                            (*Pause*. SIDMOUTH *looks into*
                            the shadows at SUSAN
                            THISTLEWOOD'S *rope*)
                  It's Susie Thistlewood. You see, my Lord.
                  Yes, she's still jerking.
LORD SIDMOUTH:But very faint.
                            (*Pause*)
                  What a strong neck.
HERBERT: .   D'you want their heads displayed,
                  my Lord?
LORD SIDMOUTH:Perhaps.
                            (*Pause*)
HERBERT: (*to* EDWARDS) Alderman Wood has pro-
                  ceedings against you.
EDWARDS: Oh yes?
LORD SIDMOUTH:Yes. They are gone out of a very trouble-
                  some world, George. Alderman Wood
                  has raised questions in Parliament on
                  your behalf.
EDWARDS: I must leave the country immediately.
LORD SIDMOUTH:You must.
HERBERT: Adams told us you lay with Mrs. Thistle-
                  wood.
                            (*Pause*)
EDWARDS: Not true, my Lord.
LORD SIDMOUTH:She was passionate?
EDWARDS: My Lord I said *not* true - she was

EDWARDS: passionate for her husband, Arthur.
(contd)

LORD SIDMOUTH:She's with him now. You bawdy fellow.
                           (*Pause*)

EDWARDS: So my Lord how many acres?

LORD SIDMOUTH:(*smiling at him*) A thousand acres!

HERBERT: What?

LORD SIDMOUTH:Massachusetts. Here are the deeds.
                           (LORD SIDMOUTH *hands the*
                           papers to EDWARDS)

EDWARDS: My Lord this is truly generous.

HERBERT: You said a hundred!
                           (LORD SIDMOUTH *takes out*
                           his whistle and blows it. A
                           CONSTABLE *appears*)
                           Escort Mr. Edwards to the docks. Beware
                           of loitering.

EDWARDS: (*smiling*) I am already at the borders of
                           the sea.

LORD SIDMOUTH:The strong man is mightiest alone. I am
                           pleased you overcame yourself. Shall
                           you farm?

EDWARDS: Farm and hunt.
                           (EDWARDS *laughs*)
                           (EDWARDS *looks back at the*
                           gallows)
                           If the time had been ripe, my Lord, I
                           would have tossed you that grenade.

LORD SIDMOUTH:I wonder.

EDWARDS: You wonder?

LORD SIDMOUTH:Yes. You must get to know yourself, my
                           dear. Goodbye, George, I shall miss you.
                           (EDWARDS *goes*)

LORD SIDMOUTH:(*to* HERBERT) I hanged his father you

LORD SIDMOUTH: know. Pray Reverend.
(contd)

(*The* REVEREND *does so*)

LORD SIDMOUTH: (*smiling*) Herbert! To what are the temporal evils which now afflict our country to be traced? Undoubtedly to apostacy in Religion, and to the alarming growth of deism and infidelity. Yes it is to the progress of irreligion and decay of morals, that the increase of crime which now stigmatises the country, indeed the world, is to be attributed. The Christian is not only obliged by his profession to be a good man, but also to be a good citizen. No subtlety of reasoning, nor any perversion of language or texts of Scripture will countenance him in acts of rebellion. To the Atheist and the Infidel let the blood of these men speak forever. Let those that doubt me, think. Think! Order. We need order. Stability! We need stability.

(LORD SIDMOUTH *smiles*)

Herbert, I shall be wanting to see Robert Adams.

(LORD SIDMOUTH *walks to the scaffold and mounts the ladder. To the* DOCTOR)

Well done, Doctor. Democracy is only possible in a brute or explosive state, eh?

(LORD SIDMOUTH *looks down into the trap.*)

I am one of the old shirts. My position derives from my English tradition and

LORD SIDMOUTH: my faith. To tell the truth when I am
(contd)   alone, I am not much interested in
                           doctrinal points.

> (LORD SIDMOUTH *laughs,*
> *holds his torch above the*
> *trap and peers down into it*)

It is me who gives you stability - it is
Sidmouth who feeds the poor.
Ding Dong.

> (LORD SIDMOUTH *rises up*
> *straight, holds his torch high,*
> *looks at the audience*)

Life's a tangled skein, dear friends, and
ravelled - but when you have a dispas-
sionate moment visit their graves, and
reflect. (*he smiles ironically*) If you
have the time. Are you still on your
knees Reverend?

REV. COTTON: Yes, my Lord.

LORD SIDMOUTH: Help the "Doctor" cut them down and
                           put them into the lime.

> (LORD SIDMOUTH *laughs*)

REV. COTTON: (*rising*) May we spare them the quarter-
                           ing, my Lord?

LORD SIDMOUTH: Why not?

REV. COTTON: Thank you, my Lord.

DOCTOR: And their heads?

LORD SIDMOUTH: Their heads?

> (*Pause*)

Yes, you had best decapitate them,
and display their heads.

HERBERT: In the churches.

LORD SIDMOUTH: No. In the market place.

> (*Pause*)

LORD SIDMOUTH:Well, Herbert, back to the Home Office.
(contd)   .

THE CURTAIN FALLS.